WRITERS AND THE

ISOBEL ARMSTR
General Edit

LAURENCE STERNE

'FRAMING STERNE'

from a crayon portrait by Wilhelm Föckersperger after the painting by Sir Joshua Reynolds

LAURENCE STERNE

MANFRED PFISTER

Northcote House
in association with the
British Council

© Copyright 2001 by Manfred Pfister

First published in 2001 by Northcote House Publishers Ltd, Horndon, Tavistock, Devon, PL19 9NQ, United Kingdom.
Tel: +44 (01822) 810066 Fax: +44 (01822) 810034.

British Library Cataloguing-in-Publication Data
A catalogue record for this book is available from the British Library

ISBN 0-7463-0837-X

Typeset by PDQ Typesetting, Newcastle-under-Lyme
Printed and bound in the United Kingdom

Contents

Acknowledgements

Laurence Sterne was one of my first literary passions when I began to discover English literature for myself in the early 1960s. Since then, reading Sterne has always been a case of 'Thou art the man!' (S 31) with me. I am, therefore, particularly grateful to Isobel Armstrong for having provided me with an opportunity to write down at long last what I find so remarkable about him.

I owe further debts of gratitude to the Freie Universität Berlin for having granted me a sabbatical, to my students of two recent seminars on Laurence Sterne for their illuminating enthusiasm, to my secretary, Frau Barbara Wohlgemuth, and my student assistants Sabine Müller and Karen Schneeweiß for their painstaking bibliographical and editorial help, and – last but not least – to Dr Indira Ghose for many helpful suggestions stylistic and otherwise.

The book is dedicated to Dominik, who may find Sterne's medical lore – as well as his father's passion for Tristram and Yorick – intriguing.

Biographical Outline

<table>
<tr><td>1713</td><td>Laurence Sterne conceived at Dunkirk, in utero while the Treaty of Utrecht is signed, born first child to Roger and Agnes Sterne on 24 November at Clonmel, Tipperary, where his father, an army ensign, was stationed at the time.</td></tr>
<tr><td>1723–31/2</td><td>At school in Hipperholme, Yorkshire.</td></tr>
<tr><td>1731</td><td>Father dies at Port Antonio, Jamaica.</td></tr>
<tr><td>1733–7</td><td>Studies at Jesus College, Cambridge, a high church college, where his great-grandfather Dr Richard Sterne had been Master during the Civil War before becoming Archbishop of York; beginning of a life-long friendship with John Hall-Stevenson, whose circle of humorous 'Demoniacs' he will join in Yorkshire; first attack of pulmonary tuberculosis; receives BA, is ordained and appointed assistant curate at St Ives.</td></tr>
<tr><td>1738</td><td>Becomes vicar of Sutton-on-the-Forest near York, where he takes his lodgings near the minster, acquiring a certain notoriety as womaniser.</td></tr>
<tr><td>1741</td><td>Preferred to prebendary in the minster; marries Elizabeth Lumley, cousin to the famous bluestocking Elizabeth Montagu; contributes several essays to his uncle Dr Jaques Sterne's new pro-Walpole York Gazetteer representing the Whig or Ministerial interest.</td></tr>
<tr><td>1742</td><td>Break with Jaques Sterne due to election politics; having alienated his uncle, Sterne withdraws from politics. Dr Sterne will blacken his reputation for the rest of his life, particularly as to the alleged uncharitable treatment of mother and sister.</td></tr>
</table>

1743	Publishes 'The Unknown World: Verses Occasioned by hearing a Pass-Bell' in the *Gentleman's Magazine*; his marriage shows increasing signs of stress.
1744	Is granted a second living as vicar of Stillington, adjacent to Sutton-on-the-Forest, and purchases Tindal Farm.
1745–6	Attacks the Roman Catholic gentry and other sympathizers with the Jacobite invasion of England, amongst them the physician Dr John Burton.
1747	His sermon 'The Case of Elijah and the Widow of Zerephath' preached in York and published; Lydia, only surviving child, born.
1749	Controversy within York Minster breaks out and pits Sterne against Jaques Sterne and Archbishop Hutton.
1750	Preaches 'The Abuses of Conscience' at the annual assizes at York Minster and has it printed.
1756	Enclosure Act nearly doubles the value of his living.
1759	Publishes *A Political Romance*, a satirical attack on the machinations of the church lawyer Dr Francis Topham, and writes 'A Fragment in the Manner of Rabelais'; his mother dies and his wife has a mental breakdown, believing herself to be Queen of Bohemia; begins affair with singer Catherine Fourmantel; has first two volumes of *Tristram Shandy* printed in York in December, half of the copies sent to London.
1760	Is lionized in London, meets Garrick and has his portrait painted by Reynolds; London edition of *Tristram Shandy*, vols. 1 and 2, with frontispiece by Hogarth, and two volumes of *The Sermons of Mr Yorick* appear in print; returns to Yorkshire to take up his new living at Coxwold ('Shandy Hall') presented to him by Lord Fauconberg.
1761	In London again for the publication of *Tristram Shandy*, vols. 3 and 4 in January; vols. 5 and 6 appear in December.
1762	Is lionized in Paris and meets the Baron d'Holbach, Buffon, Diderot and d'Alembert; suffers a lung haemorrhage and settles with family in Toulouse for health reasons.

1763   Seeks health in Bagnères-de-Bigorre and Montpellier.

1764   Leaves the family in the South of France and returns to England via Paris, where he meets John Wilkes and David Hume and preaches before the English ambassador to France. Back home in York falls in love with Sarah Tuting.

1765   *Tristram Shandy*, vols. 7 and 8, published in January; sets out after another haemorrhage on a tour to the South, which takes him as far as Naples; is painted by Thomas Patch in Florence and sculpted by Joseph Nollekens in Rome.

1766   *The Sermons of Yorick*, vols. 3 and 4, published in January; returns to England.

1767   Tristram Shandy, vol. 9, published in January; falls in love with Eliza Draper and writes *Journal to Eliza* and *A Sentimental Journey*. Wife and daughter move back to Yorkshire.

1768   Dies in London 18 March, three weeks after publication of *A Sentimental Journey* – his last words: 'Now it is come'.

Abbreviations

The following abbreviations have been used:

TS Laurence Sterne, *The Life and Opinions of Tristram Shandy, Gentleman*, ed. Melvyn and Joan New, intro. Christopher Ricks (Harmondsworth: Penguin Classics, 1997) – the reference will give the volume, chapter and page number

SJ Laurence Sterne, *A Sentimental Journey with The Journal to Eliza and A Political Romance*, ed. Ian Jack (Oxford: The World's Classics, 1984)

S *The Sermons of Laurence Sterne*, ed. Melvyn New, The Florida Edition of the Works of Laurence Sterne, vol. 4 (text). (Gainesville: University of Florida Press, 1996)

L *Letters of Laurence Sterne*, ed. Lewis Perry Curtis (Oxford: Clarendon Press, 2nd edn 1965)

CH *Sterne: The Critical Heritage*, ed. Alan B. Howes (London: Routledge & Kegan Paul, 1974)

EMY Arthur H. Cash, *Laurence Sterne: The Early and Middle Years* (London: Routledge, 1992)

LY Arthur H. Cash, *Laurence Sterne: The Later Years* (London: Routledge, 1992)

1

Swiftly Sterneward

Laurence Sterne was, after Shakespeare, the second English writer to become a European cult figure. Where it took Shakespeare, however, nearly one and a half centuries to enter the canon of European literature, Sterne's success was instantaneous. His two main books, *The Life and Opinions of Tristram Shandy, Gentleman* (1759–67) and *A Sentimental Journey* (1768) were available in other European languages only a few years after their English publication: the first German translation of *Tristram Shandy* began to appear in 1763 and the first French and the first Dutch translation in 1776; Johann Joachim Christoph Bode's celebrated translation of the *Sentimental Journey, Yoricks empfindsame Reise*, came out in the same year as the original and Joseph Pierre Frénais's *Voyage sentimental* the year after – the Italians had to wait a bit longer, before they got, after undistinguished translations from the French in 1792 and from the original in 1812, Ugo Foscolo's classic *Viaggio Sentimentale* in 1813.

The promotion of Sterne to the ranks of what Goethe was to call 'Weltliteratur' (world literature) actually coincided with that of Shakespeare, and this not only timewise but also in terms of aesthetic motivation. Sterne himself was very much aware of entering France in the footsteps of his great compatriot, who had, like him, mingled tears with laughter and broken all established rules, and he dramatizes this awareness in the 'Passport' episode of the *Sentimental Journey*, when he has his Yorick admitted to polite French society and given a French passport on the credit of his Shakespearean namesake (*SJ* 109–10). In Germany as well the adoption of Shakespeare by the Romantic poets and thinkers was closely linked with a fervent passion for Sterne. They discovered not only, with Coleridge, 'a

1

smack of Hamlet' in themselves, but just as much a smack of Sterne's Yorick and Tristram.[1]

There seems to be a paradox at work here, one of the many paradoxes that riddle Sterne's work and its reception, as we shall see: Sterne's work, in spite of – or is it because of? – what appears to be the quintessential Englishness of its eccentricity and humour, its changeability rivalling the English weather, and the liberties it takes, proved to be more at home abroad than at home. To be sure, there were followers of Sterne in England, but they were mere imitators and produced little more than feeble parodies, pastiches or sequels of the *Life and Amours of Hafen Slawkenbergius* (1762) variety. On the Continent, however, in addition to and beyond similar ephemera, Sterne's works triggered truly creative responses from major writers. Denis Diderot's *Jacques le Fataliste* (1771–4) is a first brilliant example of such a creatively critical intertextual dialogue;[2] the dialogue is continued in the novels of German Romanticists, in particular those of Jean Paul Richter and E. T. A. Hoffmann, and has not reached its end in Viktor Shklovsky's Russian *Sentimental Journey* of 1923.

That this applies to criticism as well is amply demonstrated in Alan B. Howes's 'Critical Heritage' anthology which traces the English and international reception of Sterne till 1830. The first incisive comments upon his work – apart, of course, from Sterne's own – came from foreign, not British critics. The most authoritative English critic of Sterne's time, Dr Johnson, had very little to say about him and was proved famously wrong when he prognosticated his critical fortunes in 1776: 'Nothing odd will do long. *Tristram Shandy* did not last' (*CH* 219). While the critical debate in England still continued to be mainly negative, blaming Sterne for wilfully bewildering his readers, for a bawdiness particularly unseemly for a clergyman and for his plagiaristic pilfering of sources, the Continental debate soon opened up more constructive perspectives beyond such mainly moral considera-tions. Friedrich von Blankenburg, for instance, in an early *Essay on the Novel (Versuch über den Roman,* 1774) contrasted Sterne's fictions illuminatingly with those of Richardson and Smollett, and analysed *Tristram Shandy* in terms of a distinction between 'humorists of the heart' and 'humorists of the intellect' (*CH* 385). Diderot in 1762 already defined Sterne's work-in-progress as a 'universal satire' and compared it to Rabelais: 'This book so mad, so wise, and so gay is the English Rabelais' (*CH* 393). For Voltaire it even was 'clearly superior to Rabelais', and he found a metaphor that aptly describes its structure: 'It resembles those ancient little vases decorated with satyrs which contained precious essences' (*CH* 390).

With Romanticism, the gap between English and Continental criticism of Sterne even widened. The few English Romantics who had anything relevant to say about him beyond adulation of his tender sentiments and benign humour (William Hazlitt) or denigration of his character (Byron) were almost always directly influenced by German Romantic aesthetics. Thus, Coleridge's definition of Sterne's humour as an attitude in which 'the little is made great, and the great little, in order to destroy both, because all is equal in contrast with infinity' (*CH* 354) is hardly more than a paraphrase of Jean Paul Richter's *Vorschule der Ästhetik* (1804). And De Quincey's discussion of Sterne's 'blending, or fusing [of] the elements of pathos and of humour, and composing out of their union a third metal *sui generis*' (*CH* 369) is cast, to start with, as part of an assessment of the allegedly superior quality of Jean Paul Richter's romantic irony.

Friedrich Schlegel's concepts of 'romantic irony' and the 'arabesque' (*CH* 445–6) opened up a new understanding of the seriousness of the games Sterne plays in his fictions and of his systematically digressive, frame-breaking and fragmentary narrative strategies. This turns what Sterne, in a letter of 1759, had called his 'Cervantic humour [...] of describing silly and trifling Events, with the Circumstantial Pomp of great Ones' (*L* 77) into an instance of romantic 'Universalpoesie' *avant la lettre*, which, in the face of an unrepresentable infinite, ironically subverts all distinctions of great and small, comic and tragic, completion and incompletion. That this recasting in a romantic mould occurs to Cervantes, one of Sterne's models, simultaneously with Sterne himself, is surely no coincidence. The German Romantics admired Sterne more for his ironic wit and agile intelligence than for the tender benevolence of his sentiments, and in this they agreed, for once, with Goethe.

Goethe had come to Sterne early in his literary career and, when he reread him toward the end of it, he celebrated him as a 'free soul' ('eine freie Seele'), as 'the first to raise himself and us from pedantry and Philistinism', as 'the most beautiful spirit that ever lived', 'a model in nothing and a guide and stimulator in everything' (*CH* 433–5). From here runs – via Schopenhauer, another admirer of Sterne's intellectual boldness and originality – a direct thread to Nietzsche toward the end of the nineteenth century. The subtitle of Menschliches, Allzumenschliches (Human, All Too Human, 1886) already harks back to Goethe's characterization of Sterne Ein Buch für freie Geister (A Book for Free Spirits) – and, in the section dedicated to Sterne, Nietzsche makes the connection explicit:

> How, in a book for free spirits, should there be no mention of Laurence Sterne, whom Goethe honoured as the most liberated spirit of his century! Let us content ourselves here simply by calling him the most liberated spirit of all time, in comparison with whom all others seem stiff, square, intolerant and boorishly direct.

Even if this celebration is very much an idealized self-portrait of the philosopher, it points up with great precision Sterne's aesthetic and intellectual achievement: the 'endless melody' – as Nietzsche puts it in Wagnerian terms – 'in which the fixed form is constantly being broken up'; the 'great master[y] of *ambiguity*', that does not exhaust itself in sexual innuendo but enacts a sharp-witted scepticism and 'knows how, and even wants to be in the right and in the wrong at the same time, to knot together profundity and farce'; his 'attitude of irony towards all sententiousness' united with 'a tendency to be unable to regard anything merely superficially'. To read Sterne this way is, for Nietzsche, not only a mental, but a psychosomatic experience 'closely related to floating' and induces 'a free-spiritedness in every fibre and muscle of the body'.[3] Such a tonic reading of Sterne captures what Victorian readers in England with their moralizing bent missed out on. Where they still discussed the degrees of permissible licentiousness or to what extent Sterne's religious and moral sentiments were sincere or hypocritical and more often than not found, as Thackeray did most notoriously in 1851, in every page of Sterne's writings 'a latent corruption – a hint, as of an impure presence', the 'foul Satyr's eyes leer out of the leaves constantly',[4] here we have a reading that points forward to our own concerns.

With little exaggeration one could argue that Sterne's fictions were discovered for Modernism, and for what they are and do, in Budapest in 1911 and in St Petersburg in 1921. I am referring to Georg Lukács's dialogue on Laurence Sterne, 'Riches, Chaos and Form', which explores with great subtlety Sterne's games and their limits,[5] and to Viktor Shklovsky's 'Stylistic Commentary' on *Tristram Shandy*, reprinted in revised form in 1929 as an analysis of *Tristram Shandy* as a 'parodying novel'.[6] By systematically elaborating its various devices of 'defamiliarizing' or 'making strange' conventional representations of reality – the displacement of chapters, the time-shifts, the fragmentation, the heterogeneity of materials and quotations 'knotted' together – Shklovsky reads *Tristram Shandy* as a self-reflexive novel that constantly 'lays bare' or 'foregrounds' its own textuality and the conventions of fiction. In this reading, *Tristram Shandy* is the parody of a novel rather than a novel. As such, in its highlighting the novel's rules and norms by systematically disrupting or subverting them, it appears to Shklovsky as, paradoxically, 'the most typical novel of world literature'.[7] What had been seen before as an irritating eccentricity within the history of the English novel now occupies a central place within its canon: hardly has the novel evolved in the works of Defoe, Fielding, Smollett and Richardson as a genre in its own right, when it finds its culminating parody in Sterne. What is more, for Shklovsky, Sterne's fictions belong as much with the eighteenth-century novel as with the international avant gardes of Modernism – he actually likens *Tristram Shandy* to a painting by Picasso.

My title for this introductory chapter, 'Swiftly Sterneward', is meant to point towards this sense of Sterne straddling two contexts, his and our own period. It is taken from Joyce's *Finnegans Wake*,[8] one of the paradigmatic texts of twentieth-century Modernism (or even postmodernism *avant la lettre*), and in it Joyce links Sterne with Swift and the Menippean tradition of the eighteenth century and positions himself in relation to them. And Joyce is by no means alone among modernist writers in relating himself back to Sterne by referring to him or quoting him, using some of his devices or engaging in an inspirational and creative dialogue with him. There is – to give only a few examples – Virginia Woolf, drawing attention to Sterne's 'semi-transparent' style, his art of 'nonsensical *minutiae*', and to the ways he 'transfers our interest from the outer to the inner' and, by doing this, she draws attention to significant features of her own work.[9] There is Thomas Mann invoking Sterne as a presiding spirit over his vast mythological 'Joseph' saga:

> There is a symptom for the innate character of a work, for the category toward which it strives [...]: that is the reading matter which the author prefers and which he considers helpful while working at it. [...] Well then, such strengthening reading during the last Joseph years was provided by two books: Laurence Sterne's 'Tristram Shandy' and Goethe's 'Faust' [...] and in this connection it was a pleasure for me to know that Goethe had held Sterne in very high esteem.[10]

More recently, Milan Kundera has outlined his own literary genealogy and rooted it in narrative traditions predating the realist novel, in particular in Rabelais, Sterne and Diderot, 'the greatest experimenters of all time in the novel'.[11] For him Sterne is the inventor of the 'novel-as-a-game' that is as sceptical as his own fictions are: in *Tristram Shandy 'everything* is put in question, *everything* is put in doubt, *everything* is a game'.[12] Salman Rushdie also has paid homage to Sterne as his predecessor, bowing to his 'COCK-AND-BULL story' (*TS* IX.xxxiii.543) in 'Yorick', one of the eight stories of *East, West* (1994), and awarding him the gold medal for narrative technique while contenting himself mock-modestly with the silver medal.[13] And Harold Bloom is certainly right in pointing out that 'it cannot be accidental that so many of the best contemporary Spanish-American novels are Shandean, whether or not the particular writer actually has read Sterne'.[14]

In such intertextual dialogues, in such Shandean permeations of contemporary literature, Modernism and Postmodernism have constructed Sterne's fictions as a crucial part of their own pre-history. This appropriation is quite unique and has not happened to any of the other great novelists of the eighteenth century. We might do worse, therefore, than follow the lead of these creative writers, who – at least in Sterne's case – have from the very beginning proved to be more illuminating than the professional or academic critics. To read Sterne through Nietzsche, Shklovsky, Joyce or Kundera may take us more 'swiftly Sterneward' than listening in too intently on the moral debate about Sterne that has dominated the first one and a half centuries of his reception. Anyway, we do no longer admire Sterne for what he has been admired for so uncritically by generations of readers: his genial humour, his benevolence, the tenderness of his sympathies and sentiments. We are just no longer as sure as Hazlitt was that Uncle Toby 'is one of the finest compliments ever paid to human nature'.[15] Nor are we still scandalized by what scandalized his contemporary and so many later readers: their 'bawdy' to us is a new way of writing the body, their 'insincerity' and 'hypocrisy' the double-edged irony of a self-conscious performance, their 'plagiarism' our inter-textuality, and their 'offences' to and 'confusions' of the reader part of the strategic games of metafiction.[16]

To approach Sterne as a proto-modernist or archaeo-post-modernist and thus to focus on inter- and metatextuality, on problems of language and communication, on constructions of time and subjectivity or on the performances of identity and gender, does not mean, however, that historical scholarship or scholarly criticism on Sterne as a writer of the mid-eighteenth century should be disregarded. Where such reconstructions of Sterne's original contexts have been illuminating and have stimulated a new interest in his work, they have actually converged on precisely such questions. It is easier – no, it can be a richer and more rewarding experience – to read Sterne now than in Victorian times both because we can read him with the awareness and in the light of modernist and postmodern aesthetic practices and because recent scholarship has provided us with philologically more reliable texts and a deeper knowl-edge of his relatedness to his own times.

And again, one has to say that Sterne has been more at home with scholars abroad than with British scholars. The first truly scholarly edition, *The Works of Laurence Sterne* in twelve volumes was produced by an American, Wilbur L. Cross, in 1904 and the transatlantic provenance of the new, indispensable, yet still incomplete and, alas, unaffordable 'Florida Edition' (1978–) under the general directorship of Melvyn New is proclaimed already in its name. The editor of the standard *Letters* (1935), Lewis Perry Curtis, is also an American and so are the authors of the first scholarly biography, *The Life and Times of Laurence Sterne* (1909; 3rd edn 1929), again Wilbur L. Cross; of the first critical and fully annotated editon of *Tristram Shandy* (1940), James A.

Work; of the path-breaking critical reassessment of Sterne not as a novelist, but as a brilliant and profound rhetorical juggler with the philosophical notions of his – and our – time, John Traugott (*Tristram Shandy's World: Sterne's Philosophical Rhetoric*, 1954); and of the standard biography in two volumes, *Laurence Sterne: The Early and Middle Years* (1975) and *The Later Years* (1986), Arthur H. Cash.[17] Why this *translatio imperii* of academic Sterne studies in the twentieth century should have occurred is difficult to account for, as the reception of Sterne in eighteenth- and nineteenth-century America was no less riddled with moral animadversions than in England. On the English side, it may have had something to do with the reinforcement of Victorian misgivings in the agenda-setting critical project of F. R. Leavis and his school. When he constructed his *Great Tradition* (1948), he relegated Sterne from the canon of what has been important in English fiction, dismissing his work in a curt footnote as 'irresponsible (and nasty) trifling'.[18]

I am, of course, not suggesting that the British contribution to Sterne studies is altogether negligible. There has been a moral and aesthetic revaluation, setting in, perhaps, with Herbert Read's introduction to his edition of *A Sentimental Journey*,[19] and one finds quite a number of excellent chapters on Sterne in monographs of a wider scope, such as John Preston's *The Created Self: The Reader's Role in Eighteenth-Century Fiction* (1970), A. D. Nuttall's *A Common Sky: Philosophy and the Literary Imagination* (1974) or Janet Todd's *Sensibility* (1986),[20] but there is no substantial study that could compare with the major American contributions or with Henri Fluchère's monumental *Sterne, de l'homme à l'oeuvre* (1961).[21] In this context, it seems also significant that in the two best-known anthologies of 'essential articles' on Sterne, the American contributions completely outnumber the British (and this not only because both editors hail from the States!). In both John Traugott's 'Twentieth Century Views' collection (1968) and Melvyn New's 'New Casebook' (1992) only one English article is singled out as essential. And in both cases it is the same: D. W. Jefferson's seminal study of *'Tristram Shandy* and the Tradition of Learned Wit' (1951). It was the first to deflect critical attention from *Tristram Shandy* as a novel and to redirect it toward Sterne's roots in scholastic and humanist learning and he has thus opened the way for later studies, as for instance those of Northrop Frye, who illuminated Sterne's fictions by relating them to genres such as the debate, the 'anatomy' or the Menippean satire.[22]

And D. W. Jefferson, Professor of English at Yorkshire's University of Leeds until his retirement in 1977, happened to be also the author of the volume on Sterne in the original 'Writers and their Work' series[23] – a predecessor who stirs feelings of admiration as well as anxiety in the present writer. He has set up a model that is difficult to surpass even with the help of more recent research and of the new theoretical frames which poststructuralism in its various guises has provided. The latter has not yet really risen to the Shandean occasion, anyway: where Richardson's novels in particular have gained spectacularly from deconstructivist, feminist or New Historicist readings, Sterne's fictions have – apart from a few inroads in gender studies – been largely and surprisingly bypassed by theories for which they seem to have been written.[24]

2

Life and Opinions

Laurence Sterne's first known publication is, significantly, his own name. As he tells us in a brief biographical outline written for his beloved daughter Lydia and printed by her under the title 'Memoirs of the Life and Family of the Late Rev. Mr. Laurence Sterne' in 1775 (*L* 1–5), he publicized it on the ceiling of his Yorkshire schoolroom:

> I [...] cannot omit mentioning this anecdote of myself, and schoolmaster – He had the cieling [sic] of the school-room new white-washed – the ladder remained there – I one unlucky day mounted it, and wrote with a brush in large capital letters, LAU. STERNE, for which the usher severely whipped me. My master was very much hurt at this, and said, before me, that never should that name be effaced, for I was a boy of genius, and he was sure I should come to preferment – (*L* 4)

This writing on the wall is telling for Sterne's later publications, both in the divided response it elicited as punishable transgression or sign of genius, and in the author's flamboyant gesture of self-advertising. It anticipates what, writ large, was going to be Sterne's express intention when it came to publishing the first instalment of *Tristram Shandy* in 1759/60: 'I wrote not [to] be *fed*, but to be *famous*' (*L* 90). And even if he refrained from putting his name to it, he could not renounce the pleasure of publicizing his authorship on a second title-page to *The Sermons of Mr. Yorick* a few months after the appearance of *Tristram Shandy*, vols. 1 and 2: 'Sermons by Laurence Sterne, A.M. Prebendary of York, and Vicar of Sutton-on-the-Forest, and Stillington near York' (*LY* 40). This gave away the authorship of *Tristram Shandy* as well and added notoriety to fame: it added the notoriety of a veritable vicar donning the fool's cap on the title-page of his sermons and not only writing, but actually publishing and publicly acknowledging salaciously bawdy fiction, to the fame of a wittily original and spirited new man of letters, which Sterne, arriving with his book in London, had gleefully harvested with the high and mighty. The country parson's success on the London scene was instantaneous. Indeed, he might have said with Byron after the publication of the first two parts of *Childe Harold's Pilgrimage*: 'I awoke one morning and found myself famous'. And, like him, he proved to be such a brilliant performer of his own self, that he managed to sustain his fame – and notoriety – for the rest of his life and beyond.

Sterne is at the beginning of a new phase in the history of literary authorship in England, which will culminate in figures such as Lord Byron or Oscar Wilde and extends beyond them into our century. In this version of authorship the life is no longer the private concern of the author hidden behind the work, as it was with Shakespeare, for instance, but is displayed together with it, and in it. In such romantic self-fashioning and in the spectacular self-display of the dandy or the *poète maudit*, life and work are staged as one public performance, the one reflecting and authenticating the other and the life forming a kind of *Gesamtkunstwerk* of which the work is only a part. In short, with Sterne we enter the world of literary stardom and celebrity that is still with us.

The 'self-conscious' and 'dramatized' narrators (Wayne C. Booth) of *Tristram Shandy* and of *A Sentimental Journey* constantly and intriguingly suggest the author and the sermons' two title-pages actually short-circuit the fictional and the real author. This effect is further enhanced by the many, quite transparent autobiographical references in the works. They are dispersed across his characters and suggest clear, albeit instable, equations: Sterne both is and is not Tristram, Yorick is and is not Sterne... Sterne even signed some of his letters 'Tristram' or 'Yorick', and his *Journal to Eliza* pointedly reverses the conventions of the eighteenth-century epistolary novel: instead of presenting fictional letters as real ones, it turns – with a knowing wink – true letters into fiction. His works, as they appeared in their various instalments, were not to be had without him. In the same way in which Mrs Shandy was to go to London to give birth to her children, Sterne went there annually each winter to see his new volumes delivered, to present them and himself to the literary world and the London society, and to have himself lionized. To increase his visibility, he engaged the services of other stars, of a Garrick or a Reynolds[1] or a Hogarth, and his ritually repeated public performances as country parson and author, as Yorick and Tristram, were so engagingly witty and charming that they even won him – if only for a while – the admiration and public support of so stern a critic and moralist as William Warburton, Bishop of Gloucester. And, as his fame spread to the Continent, he made Paris the stage of similar performances to an admiring audience and turned his Grand Tour to Naples into a series of star appearances. At that time he enjoyed already such celebrity that – as he boasted with a characteristic onomastic emphasis – a letter addressed simply to 'Tristram Shandy, Europe' would reach him without delay.[2]

Clearly, the writing on the wall had come true, even if fairly late in his life. For, as a literary author, Sterne was a late-starter, having already reached the age of 46 when he began to write *Tristram Shandy* in 1759. In that, he is not unlike Richardson, who was 51 when he published his first novel, *Pamela*, or Defoe, who began *Robinson Crusoe* at 59. In contrast to these, however, who arrived at writing fiction after long careers in journalism and non-fictional publication, Sterne had written very little, and published even less, before embarking upon *Tristram Shandy.*[3] Of course, like any educated person in the eighteenth century, he had written letters, but those before the *annus mirabilis* of 1759 – at least those preserved – are fairly undistinguished and do not give away literary pretensions. And, of course, as an Anglican clergyman, he had written and preached his weekly sermons ever since his ordination in 1737, and had seen two of them printed in 1747 and 1750, but they are neither doctrinally nor stylistically in any remarkable way different from so many others preached by his confrères – nor would Sterne, as their most recent editor underlines, have wished them in any way to be otherwise.[4] There was also a brief flutter of local political journalism and polemics in 1742 and, more importantly, in the very year in which he began work on *Tristram Shandy*, in 1759, there were two attempts at Rabelaisian satire; one, *A Political Romance* addressing itself to conflicts of interest within the chapter of York Minster, published successfully, the other, 'A

Fragment in the Manner of Rabelais' on the art of preaching, unearthed posthumously by his daughter in 1775.

All this does not amount to very much, and as much as scholars have tried to persuade us of the opposite, its interest is hardly intrinsic. And its extrinsic interest as preparative to the *magnum opus* can easily be exaggerated. To be sure, there are thematic, material and structural links: the concern with the narrow world of local ecclesiastical politics or with the Catholic menace to the religious and political establishment provides a link with the later work. One of the two printed sermons, 'The Abuses of Conscience' actually makes it into *Tristram Shandy* (II.xvii) with great effect, and the *Political Romance* and the 'Fragment' anticipate certain generic structures such as allegory and parodic debate, satire on pedantic learning and travesty's transposition of big into small. To construct this, however, into an evolutionary teleology can only obfuscate what is more striking, more important: the *coup de théâtre* with which Sterne exploded upon the literary scene in 1759/60 and the bursts of creativity that sustained him until his death in less than a decade.

But there is one aspect of continuity I would like to highlight: all his writing previous to *Tristram Shandy* was in genres emphatically 'performative' – 'performative' in the sense of being staged for an audience which is constantly taken into account and appealed to, a self-presentation that involves or suggests the writer's or speaker's body and voice, foregrounds the process of articulation and conveys the impression of unpremeditated spontaneity. These conditions apply to both letters and sermons, polemics and satire. Letters are by their very nature directed towards an addressee and combine what classical rhetorics had called the *ethos* of projecting a self with the *pathos* of soliciting emotional responses or moral reactions in the recipient. And even if most of the pre-*Tristram* letters – as, for instance, the long letter in which he tries to justify the alleged disregard for his mother's needs to his estranged uncle, Dr Jaques Sterne (*L* 32–41) – tend to be more formal, some of them already motion towards that 'conversational' quality which will be one of the hallmarks of the *Tristram* style from the beginning: 'Writing, when properly managed, (as you may be sure I think mine is) is but a different name for conversation' (*TS* II.xi.88).

Sermons are even more immediately performative, being written not primarily to be read but to be quite literally performed, to be delivered in front of, and to, a congregation whom they are intended to move and persuade. There is something intrinsically theatrical about preaching and something intrinsically histrionic about the preacher. And, indeed, Sterne advertised the publication of his sermons as 'The *Dramatic* Sermons of Mr. Yorick' in the *York Courant* in 1760 (my emphasis; *LY* 41; cf. also *TS* VI.xi.355) and has Walter Shandy praise Yorick's sermon in Trim's moving delivery as 'dramatic': 'I like the sermon well, replied my father, – 'tis dramatic, – and there is something in that way of writing, when skilfully managed, which catches the attention' (*TS* II.xvii.114). What Walter's phrasing acknowledges here is that this performative quality does not reside in the delivery alone but has inscribed itself into the very 'way of writing', from its appeals to the audience and the anticipations of their reactions to its gestural and dialogic qualities and its lively rhythm of long and short phrases, down to its punctuation suggesting vocal inflections:

> – *For we* trust *we have a good Conscience, –*
> Trust! – Trust we have a good Conscience! – Surely, you will say, if there is any thing in this life which a man may depend upon, and to the knowledge of which he is capable of arriving upon the most indisputable evidence, it must be this very thing, – whether he has a good Conscience, or no. (*S* 255–6; also *TS* II.xvii.100–101)

And this dramatic or performative way of preaching was not just Sterne's idiosyncrasy but was recommended in all the homiletic manuals of his time, as Melvyn New assures us.[5]

Finally, polemics and satire also involve theatricality, a sense of drama, in which the polemicist or satirist stages his attacks on the targets of his aggression and exposes them in their despicable ludicrousness to a well-defined – in Sterne's case a local – audience in the know. In satire of the Menippean kind, that is, satire employing allegory, narrative and defamiliarizing perspectives, this leads to vividly staged scenes, in which the satirized victims act out their follies and/or vices. Thus Sterne's 'Fragment in the Manner of Rabelais' stages for the reader dialogues and soliloquies in racy vernacular that dramatize the incongruities between homiletic theory and practice.[6] And *A*

Political Romance is cast in the form of a letter, responding to a previous open letter by the satire's main victim, the self-seeking and scheming church lawyer Dr Topham, and occasioning further letters, to which it then responds in turn. Moreover, this external dialogue frames the dialogues within the main letter, which reduce the conflicts of interest within the higher echelons of the York diocese to a burlesque scramble for a watch-coat and a pair of breeches.

Illuminating as it may be to study how Sterne's earlier writings already adumbrate the self-dramatizing, histrionic and performative qualities of his later works, they are no more than *parerga* and *paraleipomena*, to quote the title of one of the works of another philosophical admirer of his, Arthur Schopenhauer. They cannot, and should not, conceal the fact that Sterne, for a prose writer of the eighteenth century, has produced an uncommonly small *oeuvre* and had to produce it in an uncommonly short period of time. He is, basically, a one-book author, as *Tristram Shandy* and *A Sentimental Journey*, in spite of all their differences in emphasis and structure, which we are not going to disregard, are so closely related to each other in terms of genesis, style and material that they can be considered as parts of one project, one work-in-progress, one 'book'. Not only does the *Sentimental Journey* share the character of Yorick with *Tristram Shandy*, who is now promoted to the rank of protagonist and first-person narrator, it quite literally covers the same ground that the seventh book of *Tristram Shandy* had already covered, that is, France from Calais to the South. And the rest of Sterne's works – including the embarrassingly humourless and unmitigatedly sentimental *Journal to Eliza*,[7] the private record of his highly publicized infatuation with Eliza Draper during the last year of his life – is 'dross' in the stern sense defined by Ezra Pound: 'What thou lovest well remains, the rest is dross' (Canto LXXXI). The sermons and the letters, the polemical pieces and the *Journal*: we read them only because they are written by the author of *Tristram Shandy* and *A Sentimental Journey* and for the light we hope they may shed on his *magnum opus*.

This has consequences for the structure of our study of Sterne. Instead of a text-by-text design, I shall focus on Sterne's two crucial texts, drawing in the others only occasionally for comparison and contrast, and discuss these two as far as possible in terms of what they share (ch. 3) before taking them in turns (chs 4 and 5) and explore to what extent *A Sentimental Journey* is indeed Sterne's 'Work of Redemption', as he is said to have called it,[8] and involves a redirection of the work-in-progress.

Looking back from Sterne's years of fame, his life falls into roughly three phases: (1) the first two and a half decades of the fairly nomadic childhood of an army officer's son and his education at Yorkshire boarding schools and Cambridge, largely abandoned by his mother and looked after by 'more or less satisfactory surrogate fathers';[9] (2) two decades of dedicated service to the Church of England, most of it as vicar of Sutton-on-the-Forest near York, enjoying a gradually increasing local reputation for his preaching and his pastoral care, but also acquiring a notoriety for certain 'irregularities' unbecoming of a parish priest and a *pater familias*; (3) the last decade of celebrated authorship, moving between his new living at Coxwold and the wider horizons of London and the Continent and dying the lingering death of tuberculosis.

All three phases, in one way or another, play a role in *Tristram Shandy* or *A Sentimental Journey*, and this turns Sterne's fictions into a transparently autobiographical self-fashioning that was recognized as such already by his contemporaries and that distinguishes them from the novels of Defoe, Fielding or Richardson. The military world of the War of the Spanish Succession (1701–14), whose battles Uncle Toby stages *en miniature* on his bowling green until the Treaty of Utrecht puts an end both to them and to his re-enactments of them, is the very world into which Sterne was born as son to an ensign and to the daughter of a provider of army supplies stationed briefly in Ireland. The rural Yorkshire, in which he received his schooling and to which he returned as an ordained priest is also the centre of Tristram's and his family's world. York's Sterne appears transformed into Yorick, a country parson like himself, who preaches his sermons and dies, his benevolence misunderstood by his parishioners, of a broken heart. Equally, quite a number of the minor figures were read already by contemporaries as fictional ciphers referring to real characters of Sterne's clerical and gentry Yorkshire. In such a reading of *Tristram Shandy* and *A Sentimental Journey* as *romans à clef* – a reading that Sterne encouraged rather than denied – the Eugenius of both texts 'is' Sterne's friend since their student days, the rakish squire John Hall-Stevenson; Dr Slop 'is' the physician and obstetrician Dr John Burton of allegedly Jacobite leanings, his religion accordingly changed to Catholicism; Didius and Phutatorius, both appearing in the visitation dinner scene (*TS* IV.xxvi–xxix) 'are' Dr Francis Topham and Dr Jaques Sterne respectively...

Such identifications are part of a game that Sterne played with, and staged for, his readers as year after year the new instalments came out. Some of these identifications had the effect of raising expectations, attention and interest even when they never got beyond hearsay or strategically launched rumour and were never realized in the text. This was the case, for instance, when, after the publication of the first two volumes, gossip began to circulate that Sterne would send Tristram upon a grand tour in one of the next volumes, lampooning Bishop Warburton as his young hero's tutor and guide (*L* 92–6, *LY* 5–6). Nothing came of this, apart from a discarded satire on Warburton's role in a controversy over the authorship of the Book of Job, which cast the episcopal critic in the role of Satan and which Sterne read to numerous friends, and apart from a few unflattering side glances at his estranged early admirer in later volumes of *Tristram Shandy*, where an imaginary critic shouts at the narrator, 'you've splash'd a bishop' (IV.xx.245), or where the narrator, with sly impudence, lumbers one of Warburton's serious theological works with a satire by Swift and with his own book: 'for what has this book done more than the *Legation of Moses*, or the *Tale of a Tub*, that it may not swim down the gutter of time along with them?' (IX.viii.511). This shows Sterne as one of the early masters of serial publication: he knew how to exploit the time-gap between one instalment and the next for his performative purposes of creating suspense and stirring up excitement, responding to responses and staging himself as 'the author'.

With that, we have already reached the third phase of his life. And this phase is equally made present in his fictions, although the main events of *Tristram Shandy* either predate Sterne's birth (the Siege of Namur, 1695, where Uncle Toby receives his wound; the construction of the miniature fortifications in the first decade of the new century) or coincide with it (Uncle Toby's wooing of widow Wadman) or predate the writing of the book by some thirty to forty years. The narrator constantly reminds us of the *hic et nunc* of his writing (and of his readers' reading) as an ongoing process, and constantly suggests a whole contemporary world of lives and contacts (of which Bishop Warburton is only a tiny particle) as we move along with him from the late forties to the late fifties and from Yorkshire to France and back. And even where he speaks about things long past, about Uncle Toby's small-scale enactments of sieges or Walter Shandy composing his 'Tristra-paedia', they are all, as we shall see, related to the present of Tristram trying to narrate his 'Life and Opinions': they are 'hobby-horses' like his own writing and in that they function as metafictional tropes for his fictional project of coping with reality by representing it. In *A Sentimental Journey* we travel with Yorick – who had actually died in 1748 in *Tristram Shandy*! – through a pointedly contemporary France, in which – enemy country due to the Seven Years' War (1756–63) – the English traveller was required to obtain a passport (*SJ* 68), a France that is recognizably Sterne's own France, in which he had to wait upon Count Choiseul to solicit a passport for himself and his family in 1762 (*L* 163–4), and in the description of which he vies and argues with two travelogues published the year before the writing of his own book, *Travels through France and Italy* by 'Smelfungus' a.k.a. Tobias Smollett and *Letters from Italy* by 'Mundungus' a.k.a. Samuel Sharp, both 1766 (*SJ* 28–9). And then, of course, there are Yorick's repeated appeals to Eliza in the *Sentimental Journey*, which continue in the mode of fiction Sterne's highly publicized romance with Eliza Draper during the last year of his life and which, together with the ten *Letters from Yorick to Eliza* published by her in 1773, contributed towards canonizing her after his, and even more so after her death, as a sentimental cult figure (*LY* 346–7).

The shadowy presence of Eliza in *A Sentimental Journey* and her greater, yet equally wraithlike presence in *The Journal to Eliza* seems to be characteristic of the way Sterne represents women in his fictions. The world of *Tristram Shandy* is – surprisingly like that of Beckett's fictions[10] – very much a men's world: it is their ruling passions that dominate the events and command the reader's interest, and their ruling passions are never sexual. In comparison, the maids Susannah and Bridget and Aunt Dinah and a small host of other stage extras, even Mrs

Wadman and Mrs Shandy play only minor roles.[11] And in comparison with the intimate and emotionally highly charged 'male bonding' between Walter and his brother Toby, between Toby and his servant, Corporal Trim, and between both of them and Le Fever and son,[12] the conjugal relationship between Mr and Mrs Shandy seems to be strangely distanced and one of mutual vexation rather than mutual enrichment. Where Richardson in *Pamela* (1740–1) and even more so in *Clarissa Harlowe* (1747/8) had focused upon the female point of view and had taken sexuality tragically serious, here we are in a world in which sex is at best an embarrassing joke or a marital duty, at worst an 'unruly appetite' (*TS* IX.32.541). And often as Tristram invokes the spirit of Rabelais, the Rabelaisian celebration of the pleasures of the flesh seem to be almost totally absent. What the constant sexual innuendoes give away is actually not the joys of sex but anxiety over impotence. As James A. Work has put it so memorably: 'The shadow of sexual impotence hovers like a dubious halo over the head of every Shandy male, including the bull'.[13]

Now, all this seems to be a far cry from Sterne's notorious philandering, the stories circulating about the country parson's sexual escapades in York and the famous writer's highly publicized extramarital romances in London, Bath, Paris and elsewhere. There seems to be another paradox at work here: a sentimental Don Giovanni as the author of one of the rare great books about impotence, an ageing Cherubini, always enamoured of the fair sex, rehashing in his book the misogyny of the Church Fathers! In *Tristram Shandy*, it is only in the unromantic relationship between Mr and Mrs Shandy that we seem to recognize immediately some of the reality of Sterne's own sexual life, the estrangement from his wife, Elizabeth. She is actually made to share her name with Mrs Shandy, and it is telling that Mrs Shandy's first name is only mentioned once, in the elaborate contract that ascertains her strictly limited right to lie in in London (*TS* I.xv.33–5).

Yet there is a second couple that invites an autobiographical reading – Tristram and Jenny. Jenny plays a role somewhat similar to that of Eliza in *A Sentimental Journey*: like her, she is again and again appealed to by the narrator, without actually becoming part of the plot or appearing on stage. The exact nature of the romance between Tristram and his 'dear, dear

Jenny' (*TS* I.xviii.39) – whether it is a sentimental friendship 'without -' (*TS* I.xix.42) or a sexual relationship – remains wilfully and teasingly undefined for a long time. But there is one invocation of her rather late in the book which beats no longer about the bush:

> – Do, my dear *Jenny*, tell the world for me, how I behaved under one [of the disasters of life], the most oppressive of its kind which could befall me as a man, proud, as he ought to be, of his manhood -
> 'Tis enough, said'st thou, coming close up to me, as I stood with my garters in my hand, reflecting on what had *not* pass'd – 'Tis enough, *Tristram*, and I am satisfied, said'st thou, whispering these words in my ear, **** ** **** *** ******; _ **** ** **** – any other man would have sunk down to the center – (*TS* VII.xxix.428)

Whichever way we decipher these asterisks, this does not only unambiguously reveal the erotic nature of the sentimental relationship, it also links Tristram's romance with the all-pervading theme of impotence. (Tristram himself had been linked with it ever since the crushing of his nose at birth in III.xxvii and the castrating or circumcising sash-window accident in V.xix.) And it suggests that the relationship is not based on virile potency in the male nor on the misogynists' 'insatiable lust' on the part of the female. It is erotic rather than sexual, and its tenderness, mutual understanding and emotional investment make the expense of sexual energy, the actual penetration or sexual consummation a matter of little importance. This is also the pattern on which the relationship between Yorick and Eliza both in *A Sentimental Journey* and in *The Journal to Eliza* is formed, and the series of erotic frictions that Yorick experiences on his way across France, always playing with their sexual potential and always stopping short of fruition, repeat this pattern in a minor, more fleeting key.

Here we are closer to Sterne than appeared at first sight – perhaps not closer to the actual economy of his sexual desires (who could claim to know about it!), but closer at least to the way he staged them in a cult of sentimental attachments. The series of 'affaires' that make up what we know of his promiscuous love life is not altogether different from the pattern described above. Most of the women he wooed, including his wife and ending with Eliza Draper, were fragile, in need of protection or ailing, often consumptive like himself (*LY* 221). His sexual desire can thus shroud itself in the language of sympathy. Where in letters to male friends and in Latin he can lament – or boast about? – his phallic urge, his being 'mentulatior quam par est' ('unbearably horny', *L* 124), in his erotic correspondence he tends to leave the sexual nature of the relationship undefined, or translates it in playful sublimation to that between brother and sister, father and daughter, 'Bramin' and 'Bramine'. This is not mere self-delusion and hypocrisy or fear of female sexuality and male anxiety about one's own sexual performance – which it all may as well have been. More importantly, however, it tries to create a new erotic space beyond the divisions of sanctioned and illicit love and to explore forms of love-making that do not drive aggressively towards sexual congress. In this, they project a new model of masculinity as well: a masculinity that is not afraid of appearing effeminate, but actually cultivates a traditionally female sensibility, weakness and vulnerability. Love here is less a matter of taking possession of the partner than of fleeting resonances and frictions, less a matter of penetrating than touching, of genital parts than of what lies between them and the mind: vibrating emotions, the language of hands and eyes. And it delights in (fore-)play and (masturbatory) fantasy. In this sense, Sterne's fictions, playing out these fantasies, are the continuation and culmination of his love life.

There is none of them more moving – in all the senses of the word – than the story of Corporal Trim, wounded in the knee, and the young Beguine nursing him (*TS* VIII.xix–xxii):

> The fair *Beguine*, said the corporal, continued rubbing with her whole hand under my knee – till I fear'd her zeal would weary her – 'I would do a thousand times more,' said she, 'for the love of *Christ*' – In saying which she pass'd her hand across the flannel, to the part above my knee, which I had equally complained of, and rubb'd it also.
>
> I perceived, then, I was beginning to be in love –
>
> As she continued rub-rub-rubbing – I felt it spread from under her hand, an' please your honour, to every part of my frame –
>
> The more she rubb'd, and the longer strokes she took – the more the fire kindled in my veins – till at length, by two or three strokes longer than the rest – my passion rose to the highest pitch – I seiz'd her hand –
>
> – And then, thou clapped'st it to thy lips, *Trim*, said my uncle *Toby* – and madest a speech.

21

> Whether the corporal's amour terminated precisely in the way my uncle *Toby* described it, is not material; it is enough that it contain'd in it the essence of all the love-romances which ever have been wrote since the beginning of the world. (*TS* VIII.xxii.479–80)

This is a pointed reversal of gender roles, in which the male invalid contentedly plays the passive part to the young Beguine's actively, though innocently (?) eroticizing ministrations. Yet, as she is attending to his wound, the young woman's sexually stimulating massage is couched as part of the traditionally female role of nursing and healing. What could be crudely described as masturbation is promoted in Trim's account to the elevated dignity of active charity and the quintessence of romance. And, what is more, to the Beguine as the member of a lay religious sisterhood it is part of her charitable mission in the name of Jesus Christ. In this male fantasy, religion spills over into the erotic, and the core of Sterne's sentimental eroticism could indeed be described as 'spilt religion'. Whether, and where, Trim's seed is also spilt we will never know – just as we will never know how far Sterne went with 'Kitty' Fourmantel, Sarah Tuting, or Eliza Draper – as Uncle Toby interrupts, to great comic effect, though not the coitus, yet Trim's vivid re-enactment of the scene. What it demonstrates clearly, however, is what such storytelling performs: it captivates the reader as much as it prepares Toby for his own long-delayed amours, softens his *rigor Martis* and makes him vulnerable for Mrs Wadman's final assault in the following chapters.

I have lingered so long over this scene because it seems to me paradigmatic of the fusion of the erotic with benevolent sentiment, of the erotic with religion, Sterne drives at both in his life and his fictions, contrasting this fusion with a wide spectrum of attitudes towards, and performances of, human sexuality which range from scatological and obscene zest to a denigration of the body as inherently bawdy, from a Manichean condemnation of the flesh to the inevitable return of the repressed, from sinful pleasure to marital duty...[14] There is, however, a problem with this 'Anatomy of Sexuality': it is hardly in line with the theology of sex and the sexual politics of the church which Sterne represented as priest and preacher. The wedded life of the Shandys is hardly an appealing example of what the 'Sacrament of Holy Matrimony' should bring about:

they have obviously not become 'one flesh' and his 'wooing her with his body' is hardly more than the physical hygiene of periodic ejaculation and a duty fulfilled with joyless clockwork regularity. And the erotic alternatives to marriage Sterne experimented with in his life and fantasized about in his fictions are plain sinfulness even to the most latitudinarian Anglican Christian.

Of course, we do not know what Sterne 'actually' believed – who could possibly know, as one does not know that even about oneself? What we do know, however, is the belief he professed and performed in his pastoral function and his sermons as a priest of the Anglican Church, the Church of England: an orthodoxy that defined itself as the *via media*, the *media aurea* between Roman Catholicism and Puritanism (represented for Sterne in particular by the new spiritual movement of Methodism), between the tyranny of absolute papal authority and the anarchy of the individual conscience insisting upon its own absolute truth, between seeking salvation in formal observances and the spiritual pride of those who see themselves already saved, between superstition and 'enthusiasm', between pompous and empty ritual and forms of worship emptied of all ceremony.[15] Both extremes are frequently referred to and rejected in Sterne's sermons (cf. for Methodism and enthusiasm, *S* 137, 242–3, 347–8, 357–65; for Catholicism, *S* 62–3, 136–7, 184, 260, 265, 301–2, 347–56, 396), and his fictions share their anti-Catholicism, even if in *A Sentimental Journey*, in the episode with the Franciscan Father Lorenzo near the beginning, the hostile stereotype is challenged in the personal encounter and the doctrinal hostility softened by charitable and benevolent emotions.

In 'Latitudinarianism', a theological position controversially staked out by divines such as John Tillotson or Samuel Clarke in the late seventeenth century and by Sterne's times a mainstream position within the Church of England, the compromise that is Anglicanism was seeking a further reconciliation with what challenged Christianity and all revealed religion from the outside: rationalism and an Enlightenment trust in man's secular potential. Without compromising the belief in divine revelation, in the necessity of grace and faith for salvation and in the doctrine of Original Sin and the Fallen State of mankind altogether, Latitudinarianism tried to mediate between reason and revelation by reappraising human reason as a gift of God, yet still maintaining its fallibility and limitations, and emphasized man's natural capacity for goodness and virtue, which, however, due to our fallen nature, are still in constant need of religious guidance. Sterne's sermon on the 'Abuses of Conscience', which becomes Yorick's in *Tristram Shandy* II.xvii, is a good exposition of this precariously balanced theological middle ground between Catholicism and Methodism as well as between trust in reason and awareness of its limitations. Obviously, Sterne found Latitudinarianism congenial in its less doctrinal habitus, its more optimistic view of human nature and its appreciation of sympathy and social feelings, benevolence and charitable deeds rather than rigorous moral norms. One of his sermons is actually dedicated to the 'Vindication of Human Nature'. It defends the naturally social inclinations of man against grim and Puritanical views of human nature as totally corrupted by the Fall, as well as against the Hobbesian or Mandevillian denigration of human nature and the

> rough usage she has met with from the satirical pens of so many of the French writers, as well as of our own country, who with more wit than well-meaning have desperately fallen foul upon the whole species, as a set of creatures incapable either of private friendship or public spirit, but just as the case suited their own interest and advantage. (*S* 66–7)

With all its theological underpinnings, this is a philosophical and political as much as a religious position. In this stance, Sterne aligns himself with Shaftesbury and Addison, dissociating himself at the same time from the Tory satirists of the previous generation, Swift and Pope. In political terms this moderately optimistic view of man and the possibility of ameliorating social relations is Whiggish and so is Sterne's patriotic pride in the liberties achieved within the constitutions of the English state and church. As he has it in the sermon on 'The Abuses of Conscience':

> GOD and reason made the law, and have placed Conscience within you to determine, – not like an *Asiatick* Cadi, according to the ebbs and flows of his own passions, – but like a *British* judge in this land of liberty, who makes no new law, – but faithfully declares that

24

glorious law which he finds already written. (*S* 267; *TS* II.xvii.113)

And indeed, in the brief periods of his life in which Sterne meddled with politics at all, he sided with the Whigs, expecting support and promotion from them. In this context it is significant that he dedicated both the first and the last instalment to William Pitt, the great Whig statesman and orator.[16]

Sterne's sermons are latitudinarian also in their reticence about sexual morals. Eloquent as he waxes when it comes to praising active sympathy and charity and the pleasures and the happiness that go with them, he says very little about sinful desires and lust. The old Christian discourse inveighing against the evil allure of women and the sins of the flesh, which goes back to St Paul and the Church Fathers and was reinstated obsessively in certain Puritanical discourses, is completely absent from his sermons. For him, sexual morals is not the crucial issue within the scheme of Christian ethics. He does, of course, not preach a gospel of sexual permissiveness or justify promiscuity or love outside wedlock, but in the rather rare cases where he turns to such concerns he shows understanding rather than condemnation. In the beautiful sermon on 'The Levite and his Concubine' (*S* 167–76) he turns the moving story of the Levite, who is betrayed and abandoned by his concubine and wins her back through forgiveness and love (*Judges* 19:1–3), into a lesson in cultural difference – Hebrew concubines were not, he insists, prostitutes but 'differ'd little from the wife, except in some outward ceremonies and stipulations' and, like a wife, gave themselves 'with sentiments and with affection' (*S* 169) – as well as into a lesson in the virtues and values of female companionship –

> Let the torbid Monk seek heaven comfortless and alone – GOD speed him! For my own part, I fear, I should never so find the way: let me be wise and religious – but let me be MAN: wherever thy Providence places me, or whatever be the road I take to get to thee give me some companion in my journey, be it only to remark to, How our shadows lengthen as the sun goes down; – to whom I may say, How fresh is the face of nature! How sweet the flowers of the field! How delicious are these fruits! (*S* 170)

– and, finally, a lesson against rash and self-righteous censuring (*S* 175–6). And as much as this sermon is indebted to the

Anglican homiletic tradition – here in particular Bishop Joseph Hall's *Contemplations* (1612–26, cf. Notes to *The Sermons of Laurence Sterne*[17]) – down to its very phrasing, we cannot but hear a note of *Apologia pro vita sua* here, as the Levite translates all too easily into the parson of Coxwold – or if it comes to that, into the Yorick of *A Sentimental Journey*.

In spite of all latitudinarian magnanimity, Sterne's sermons are, of course, doctrinally orthodox and consistent and they do draw lines beyond which promiscuity or extramarital sex are identified as sin and transgression. It would, however, be wrong to take this doctrinal framework as the blueprint of his fictions, to measure them – as some critics have done[18] – against the norms and values projected in the sermons and to posit then a satirical and vituperative intention, whenever the fictions represent attitudes, sentiments or behaviour beyond these norms. Read this way, Sterne's *Sentimental Journey* in particular becomes a grim, a stern book indeed (to take up Joyce's punning on the comic inappropriateness of Freud's, Sterne's, and his own name), turning Yorick into a 'laughing-stock' held up to ridicule by Sterne for having 'no adequate notion of true moral virtue' and for his failure 'to govern himself'.[19] As if Sterne's fiction were nothing but the translation of the moral framework of the sermons into another medium, the illustrative fleshing-out of abstract norms in characters, situations and plot! No, sermons and fictions are two different kinds of performance that cannot be translated one into the other, as they follow different rationales, are embedded in different situations and and aim at different effects. Fictions can test the very norms that sermons reiterate and try to put forward as persuasively as possible, and they can experiment imaginatively with what lies beyond these norms, act out fantasies denied or silenced in official discourses. Moreover, the concept of critical satire posited here is much too punitive and aggressive to fit Sterne's humour. As he himself has it in the very sermon on 'The Levite and the Concubine' which we have just discussed: 'there is a difference between *Bitterness* and *Saltness*' in satire, between 'the malignity and the festivity of wit', and Sterne opts for the second, 'which comes down from the Father of Spirits' and has that 'dexterity of true genius, which enables him rather to give a new colour to the absurdity, and let it pass' (*S* 175).

Sterne could afford – and exploit – such amused tolerance as well as such experimental boldness, because he saw himself living in a fairly stable world, sheltered within the Anglican Church, that tranquil fold of moderation and compromise after the traumatic religious turmoil of the seventeenth century, and in an England, since 1707 a United Kingdom, which the Bloodless or Glorious Revolution of 1688 had pacified and which had become the most libertarian, constitutionally balanced and modern state of all the major nations in Europe. In a sermon on the 'Thirtieth of January' (S 304–12), the day commemorating the execution of Charles I in 1649, he actually looks back at this history as the 'history of our deliverances, and God's blessings', a divine, providential deliverance comparable only with that of the Jews (S 307).

It is this prehistory to the contemporary political world, rather than the present itself, that is his main historical concern in his fictions as well. The contemporary historical situation in England is almost completely absent in them, only glimpsed at very occasionally: to be sure, A Sentimental Journey has a more contemporary setting, yet it is set in France, and Tristram Shandy is, as we have seen, almost historical fiction. Its main events have taken place two or three or four reigns before – in the times of William III, rising to the throne in the Glorious Revolution, of Queen Anne and of the first Hanoverian king, George I, in which Sterne's England found its present political mould. In this context, Tristram's birthday, the Fifth of November (TS I.v.10), is not accidental, but derives meaning from this construction of national history: it is part of the cultural memory that celebrated this day throughout the eighteenth century as the anniversary both of the uncovering of the Gunpowder Plot in 1605, which put an end to the Popish menace for good, and of William of Orange's arrival in England as the new king, William III, in 1688.[20]

Equally backward-looking are Sterne's fictions in their intellectual bearings and literary affiliations. In that resides another paradox: the mid-eighteenth-century writer adopted by so many modernists and postmodernists as their forerunner drew his inspiration from the past rather than his own present. We have already mentioned his debt to the latitudinarian divines of the seventeenth century, but the philosopher who presides over his fictions by providing whetstones for his wit also belongs to the late seventeenth century: John Locke and his *Essay Concerning Human Understanding* (first edition 1690). The more fashionable contemporary philosophers, in particular David Hume and his *Treatise of Human Nature* (1739–40) and Adam Smith and his *Theory of Moral Sentiment,* published less than a year before the first two volumes of *Tristram Shandy* are, on the other hand, resolutely disregarded – even though they deal with concerns immediately relevant to Sterne's own investigations into the nature of our knowledge of the world, of subjectivity and the relationship between religion and morality.

Similarly, and even more strikingly absent is contemporary literature. Sterne writes as if the 'Rise of the Novel' (Ian Watt) had never occurred; at least, he never deigns to refer to the novels of Defoe, Fielding or Smollett, or even of Richardson, either in his letters or in his fictions. (Smollett is, of course, famously poked fun at in *A Sentimental Journey,* yet not as a novelist, but a travel writer.) This disregard was actually mutual: Dr Johnson, at their one and only meeting late in 1761, snubbed him for his self-display and 'indelicate conversation' (*LY* 108–10); Richardson found the first two volumes of *Tristram Shandy* 'execrable' and refused to read more of works that had as their only extenuating circumstance 'that they are too gross to be inflaming' (*CH* 128); Goldsmith, shortly before embarking on his own sentimental novel, *The Vicar of Wakefield* (written 1761–2, published 1766), attacked him, without disgracing his own text with Sterne's name, in 'Letter liii' of his *Citizen of the World* (1760) for his 'Bawdy' and 'Pertness' (*CH* 91).

In this context, a meeting with Lord Bathurst in 1760 at the Princess of Wales's court, just after the appearance of the first instalment of *Tristram Shandy,* is of almost symbolic significance. Sterne records it in a letter to Eliza seven years later. He reminds her who this octogenarian was: 'the protector of men of wit and genius', who 'has had those of the last century, Addison, Steele, Pope, Swift, Prior, &c. &c. always at his table' and 'of whom your Popes, and Swifts, have sung and spoken so much'. And it is with great pride that Sterne records what this monument of a bygone age said to him:

> I have lived my life with geniuses of that cast; but have survived them; and, despairing ever to find their equals, it is some years since

I have closed my accounts, and shut up my books, with thoughts of never opening them again: but you have kindled a desire in me of opening them once more before I die; which I now do; so go home and dine with me. (*L* 304–5; see also *LY* 27–8)

This placed Sterne where he wanted to be: with the Augustan wits of the reigns of Queen Anne and George I at the beginning of his century. And it is from them that he learnt some of his devices and drew some of his materials and models. In Pope and Swift he found pedantic learning and religious enthusiasm already satirized and the battle between wits and dunces already staged, and in them he could study the satirical effects of vividly imagined *personae*, of image-patterns of rising and falling, inflation and deflation, or of a mock-heroic style. Swift, his brother in the cloth, he admired and envied for his bold scatological provocations: 'Swift has said a hundred things I durst Not Say – Unless I was Dean of St. Patricks' (*L* 76). Swift's allegorical *Tale of a Tub* is a direct model for the allegory in his own *Political Romance* and the *Tale*'s apparently chaotic structure may have encouraged him in *Tristram Shandy* to play similar games with digressions, and digressions within digressions, and with a narrator confusing rather than clarifying his story through constant reflections upon how to tell it. Even its basic plot, abortive as it remains, may have been suggested by a work in which Pope and Swift and other Augustan writers had a hand, *The Memoirs of Martinus Scriblerus*, first published in the prose works of Pope 1741, but written much earlier.[21] On one level at least *Tristram Shandy* repeats the 'Bildungsroman' *avant la lettre* of the *Memoirs of Martinus Scriblerus*, with Walter Shandy's encyclopaedic 'Tristrapaedia' for his son fulfilling, or rather failing to fulfil, the same role as the educational programme which the comically inept virtuoso and 'philosopher of ultimate causes', Cornelius Scriblerus, devised for his.

Of course, there remains a fundamental difference between Sterne and the Tories of a generation ago, the 'Scriblerians': Swift and Pope saw themselves threatened by a world in a terrifyingly rapid process of change and modernization, a world going down the drain – the 'Dawning of the Dunces', if not the 'Twilight of the Gods'. Accordingly, their satirical visions are apocalyptic where Sterne's satirical impulse, the 'festivity of wit', rather than castigating vice and folly and shocking with images of extreme perversion and corruption, delights in what is absurd and curious, strange and bizarre. He took some of his 'salt' from them, but did not share their 'bitterness', their dark, Hobbesian view of mankind.[22] And for some of his salt he went back even further than the Augustan wits, to the saltcellars and pickles of the preceding centuries, to Robert Burton's *Anatomy of Melancholy* (1621), to Cervantes's *Don Quixote* (1605/15), to Montaigne's *Essays* (1580/85), to Rabelais's *Gargantua and Pantagruel* (1532/34/52) and to a host of more recondite texts in the 'tradition of learned wit' (D. W. Jefferson) that link the Renaissance back to the vanishing world of medieval scholasticism and even further back to ancient Aristotelian philosophy.[23] And, paradoxically, it is in these links backwards to the Early Modern period, to the Renaissance breaking away from, yet still entangled in, medieval formations of knowledge and forms of representation that *Tristram Shandy* in particular has proved so fascinating to modernists and postmodernists. This, perhaps even more paradoxically, applies also to how Sterne's work relates to Romanticism, or rather to how Romantic writers related themselves to him. It is less – as a favourite cliché of literary historiographers has it – his famous sentimentalism or sensibility that gain him a place in their construction of 'Pre-Romanticism' than what he shares with the Early Modern traditions of learned wit: the staging of folly; the accumulation of equally vast as vain collections of curious materials, theorems and systems that turns the mind into a 'theatre of memory' and the text into a 'Wunderkammer' or a 'Kuriositätenkabinett'; the encyclopaedic anatomizing and the melancholy that goes with such self-defeating, because always incomplete, anatomies; the irony and the tragicomedy; the fragment, the arabesque, the labyrinth...[24]

3

Writing the Hobby-Horse

What kind of book did Sterne actually write? Or, what kind of book did he think he wrote? What were the generic expectations of his audience he appealed to and tried to fulfil? The standard answer to such questions has, for a long time, always been: a novel.

And, indeed, in certain respects *Tristram Shandy* and *A Sentimental Journey* are not unlike the novels of Sterne's contemporaries. Like these, they have fictional characters, whose interactions in a plausible milieu amount to a plot. In *Tristram Shandy* the story told is that of Tristram, particularly the earliest phases of his life intimately bound up with his family: how he was conceived, born, baptized, put into trousers. It is the story of a series of accidents that befall him and frustrate his father's ambitions for him: how his conception was jeopardized by an unlucky *interruptus* (*TS* I.i), how his nose was crushed and his cranium bruised at birth (*TS* III.xxvii), how he came to be baptized 'Tristram' rather than 'Trismegistus' (*TS* IV.iv), how the father's writing of the 'TRISTRA-*paedia*' proved to be counter-productive (*TS* V.xvi), how he was inadvertently circumcised by the fall of a sash window (*TS* V.xvii). And later events – the journey through France chased by Death (*TS* VII), and, also overshadowed by approaching Death, the writing of his 'Life and Opinions' (*TS* I–IX) – seem to continue this pattern of mishaps, failures and traumata. What we seem to have here, then, is the novel as the story of the life of a fictional character, the novel as fictional biography, as with Fielding's *History of Tom Jones, A Foundling* (1749), albeit with certain modifications such as the focus on the earliest phases of the protagonist's life and the deflection of the success story into one of arrested or

31

frustrated growth. Or, to apply concepts of the later history of the novel to it: a kind of *Entwicklungsroman* or *Bildungsroman*, then, albeit inverted, turned upside down, negativized?

Similarly, one could argue that *A Sentimental Journey* falls into a recognizable pattern of eighteenth-century fiction: the novel as a fictional travelogue, as the account of a crucial phase in the life of its fictional character, the *rite de passage* of a journey. That would relate it – disregarding differences in the spatial and temporal dimensions of the journeys – to, say, Defoe's *Robinson Crusoe* (1719), Tobias Smollett's *Adventures of Roderick Random* (1748) or his *Expedition of Humphrey Clinker* (1771). In them, as in *A Sentimental Journey*, the plot is a chain of events along a traveller's road, a series of encounters between self and other that are cast as educational experiences. Yorick's account of his tour across France may be more concerned with the weakness of his own heart (*SJ* 16) than with external reality and, his tour being 'a quiet journey of the heart in pursuit of NATURE' (*SJ* 84), it may be less adventurous than the other fictional journeys; still it follows the same basic pattern. And finally, the first-person narration of both *A Sentimental Journey* and *Tristram Shandy* would not have struck eighteenth-century readers as a startling departure from the conventions of the novel, nor was the self-consciousness which both Tristram and Yorick demonstrate as narrators without precedent in the contemporary novel, even though more frequently there it had been a feature of third-person narrators, such as Fielding's omniscient narrator in *Tom Jones*.[1]

So, it was novels Sterne had written, and accordingly, literary historians have accorded him a place in the history of the English novel – among its founding fathers, or among the founding fathers of the 'sentimental novel', or somewhere between them and the realist novel of the nineteenth century. But somehow his fictions would not fit into any of these *grands recits* of the triumphal march of the English novel from Daniel Defoe to Virginia Woolf, unless one provided a separate niche for him, viewing him as a parodic sideline to Fielding or as one of a discontinuous series of 'English Eccentrics'. For, as our descriptions of *Tristram Shandy* and *A Sentimental Journey* as novels should already have demonstrated, to describe them this way is to distort and reduce them, and to leave out what makes them unique and particular. He does present characters interacting with each other in a plausible ambience, but the how and the why of his representing them and the way he makes their interactions amount to something larger, a plot or an overall structure, differ significantly from the ways of the eighteenth-century novel. The differences begin with a wilfully perverse focalization that has the protagonist's life focused upon in a phase where he can hardly have any opinions and, even more bizarre, has his life and opinions totally eclipsed by everybody else's lives and opinions. And these differences do not end with a confusingly non-linear narrative chronology, which, more often than not, leads the reader backwards rather than forwards or progresses in leaps and somersaults. Moreover, and perhaps more importantly still, Sterne offers much more than character and plot – so much more that they do not seem to be, as in a novel, the *raison d'être*, the centre of his texts. Plot and character are, indeed, marginalized by constant digressions – which the epigraph to volume VII cheekily declares with Pliny to be 'opus ipsum', the very substance of the work –, by lengthy and arcane documents in various languages, by learned disquisitions on a wide variety of subjects ranging from theology to obstetrics, from epistemology and language philosophy to the science of fortifications, by stories within stories, by sermons and dialogues with the reader, by lists of odds and ends, by pages empty or marbled...

No wonder, then, that Sterne never relates his own text to the contemporary novel but, instead, again and again refers the reader back to older and more generously open and heterogeneous forms of narration (Rabelais, Cervantes) and to the holdalls of Renaissance essays (Montaigne) and anatomies (Burton), which rehashed, with a comic delight in abundance and absurdity, materials from the encyclopedic compendia of medieval theology, rhetorics, law or medicine. In consequence, a number of scholars have suggested alternative generic traditions, genres different from the novel, as more adequate or useful frames for a study of Sterne: D. W. Jefferson proposed the 'Tradition of Learned Wit' (1951),[2] John Traugott rhetorics, dialectics and philosophy (1954),[3] Northrop Frye the anatomy (1957),[4] and Melvyn New the satire (1969).[5]

These proposals are not so much at odds with each other as may appear at first sight. After all, anatomy and rhetorics are part of the tradition of learned wit, and anatomy and satire are quite closely related, if one considers the original meaning of the word 'satire', recovered for the learned world in the early seventeenth century by Isaac Casaubon. Casaubon proved that the etymological derivation of 'satire' from 'satyr', that had defined the genre as one of bitter vituperation and ridicule, of a Juvenalian – and again Swiftian – *saeva indignatio*, was actually wrong. 'Satire' instead derives from 'satura', a bowl filled brimful with all sorts of fruit, and satire under such auspices is therefore less defined in terms of aggressive ridicule than as a humorous 'gallimaufry' or 'hotchpotch', as the Elizabethans would have called it, an omnium-gatherum of themes and languages, which ridicules and celebrates the diversity and abundance there is of folly and absurdity. Frye's characteriza-tion of *Tristram Shandy* as an anatomy characterizes it, therefore, as a satura/satire at the same time:

> *Tristram Shandy* may be [...] a novel, but the digressing narrative, the catalogues, the stylization of character along 'humour' lines, the marvellous journey of the great nose, the symposium discussions, and the constant ridicule of philosophers and pedantic critics are all features that belong to the anatomy.[6]

The characters and the plot, then, also fall into their generic place: they relate Sterne's fictions less to the novel than to the allegorical devices of anatomies and to the rudimentary and fantastic plots of Menippean satire.

The mere fact, however, that Sterne, neither in his letters nor in the fictions themselves, ever referred to them as novels does not necessarily imply a dissociation from this new genre. By his time, the term 'novel' had not yet established itself for what Fielding, in the preface to *Joseph Andrews* (1742), still had to paraphrase laboriously as 'a comic-epic in prose'.[7] It is interesting, though, to attend to what Sterne actually called his fictions, to note what generic terms he used to characterize them. Here is a list of the more important ones, culled from *Tristram Shandy* and *A Sentimental Journey*: a rhapsody, i.e. an impassioned, irregular, fragmentary piece (*TS* I.xiii.31; VII.xx-viii.426); a 'history of myself' or 'my life', i.e. a form of (auto-)biography (I.iv.8; I.vi.11; I.xiv.28f); a 'book apocryphal', i.e. dubious in its status (II.viii.84); 'this cyclopaedia of arts and sciences', i.e. an anatomy (II.xvii.98); 'a careless kind of civil, nonsensical, good humoured Shandean book', i.e. something unique and in a class of its own (VI.xvii.362); 'an account of [...] my heart' (*SJ* 16), 'my travels' (*SJ* 89), 'the history of myself' (*SJ* 15). These terms point either in the direction of biography, autobiography and travel writing as forms of historiography[8] or towards the genres of learned wit. In most cases, however, he refers to his fictions simply as 'the', 'this' or 'my work', 'the', 'this', or 'my book', or 'my writing' – as if the genre he is composing in were purely and simply 'writing', *écriture*.

Writing not a novel or a romance or a satire, but writing 'writings' is a kind of writing that does not follow pre-established rules, but creates, improvises and disrupts rules as it goes along, a kind of writing that constantly draws attention to itself as an ongoing process and project, that self-consciously foregrounds what it means to write and what makes a book a book and a work a work and how they relate, say, to speaking and conversation or to visual or theatrical representations. In short, such generic writing is a performance. And, indeed, Sterne himself uses this term to characterize his own work, for instance when he refuses to 'rhapsodize' the Duke of Marlborough's campaigns 'in so flimsy a performance as this' (*TS* VI.xxi.368). Moreover, his contemporary critics, at a loss for a better word to define the genre of his fictions, frequently resorted to this term: Lady Bradshaigh thinks 'the performance [*Tristram Shandy*, vols. I and II] mean, *dirty Wit*' (*CH* 90); for an anonymous reviewer 'the whole performance' is 'blameable for [...] a general want of decorum' (*CH* 127) and another one laments that the 'novelty of the performance made many overlook the indecency' (*CH* 154). Richardson, the novelist, foretells that 'this performance' will soon be 'as much decryed, as it is now extolled' (*CH* 129) and Ralph Griffiths sees in 'so motley a performance' nothing but 'the PANTOMIME OF LITERATURE' (*CH* 181). A notice in the *Political Register* admires *A Sentimental Journey* as 'the best of the late Mr. Sterne's ingenious performances' (*CH* 201), and for Elizabeth Montagu 'Poor Tristrams [sic] last performance' also surpasses the others (*CH* 208). The inscription placed on a stone near Sterne's grave in St George's Church in 1769 commemorates 'his incomparable performances' (*CH* 209) and the unidentified editor of the first

Complete Works (1780) considered it a 'debt of gratitude, to collect his scattered performances' (*CH* 246).[9] As these examples show, 'performance' is often used dismissively here, in the derogatory sense of making an embarrassing or scandalous spectacle of oneself. But even where the term is used to belittle and decry Sterne's achievement it defines an essential quality of his writing: the sense that he performs for and to an audience, always with an eye upon it, dextrous like an acrobat, improvising wittily like a professional fool, a harlequin or a mountebank, histrionically parading his art like a virtuoso, an orator or an actor. Ralph Griffiths, despite his Puritan misgivings, puts it in a nutshell: Sterne's writing is the 'pantomime of literature' indeed.

With that I have returned to what may well prove to be my own Shandean hobbyhorse: Sterne as a performer of his own self and the performance quality, the 'performativity' of his writing. Heedful of Lodwick Hartley's warning – 'the critic who attempts to impose any kind of system on *Tristram Shandy* immediately assumes the role of Tristram's father. (This is one of the traps that Sterne himself has laid.)'[10] – I shall nevertheless pursue this perspective further, as I believe it does not only illuminate the distinctive quality of Sterne's writing but also helps to account for the enduring and recently increased interest in it. Having highlighted some of the performance aspects of Sterne's *life* in my previous chapter, of how he self-consciously staged himself on the literary scene, I am now going to explore his *writing* for their performance quality. What is it, that makes it so uniquely performative?[11]

Let me begin at the beginnings. This is how *A Sentimental Journey* begins:

> —They order, said I, this matter better in France——You have been in France? said my gentleman, turning quick upon me with the most civil triumph in the world. – Strange! quoth I, debating the matter with myself, That one and twenty miles sailing, for 'tis absolutely no further from Dover to Calais, should give a man these rights–I'll look into them. (*SJ* 3)

And, very near the beginning of *Tristram Shandy*, after a brief introduction by the narrator, we get the following:

> *Pray, my dear*, quoth my mother, *have you not forgot to wind up the clock?*——*Good G–!* cried my father, making an exclamation, but

taking care to moderate his voice at the same time,——*Did ever woman, since the creation of the world, interrupt a man with such a silly question*? Pray, what was your father saying?——Nothing. (*TS* I.i.6)

In a way, this is beginning *ab ovo*, as Tristram has it, quoting Horace, three chapters later (I.iv.8): beginning not even with the birth but with the conception of the protagonist (as if he were some mythical hero in an epic poem) or, as in *A Sentimental Journey*, beginning with the initial impulse that makes Yorick embark upon his journey. Yet, in another and more immediate sense, this is also beginning *in medias res*. We are straightaway catapulted into a situation which we do not fully comprehend as we do not know what went on before, what defines it, and what is at stake. Which matter is ordered better in France? And who is the 'I' and who 'my gentleman'? And why should an innocent question, whether the clock has been wound up by the husband or not, occasion such an outburst? With both the gentleman's and Mrs Shandy's question we have no problem understanding what the words *mean*; what escapes us, rather, is what these words *do*. In the language of 'speech-act' theory: the semantic meaning is clear, but their illocutionary force, their performative dimension remains a riddle at first and is thus highlighted from the beginning. It is only in the light of later information that we realize that 'You have been in France?' is not a question asked for curiosity's sake but a challenge, an attempted put-down, and that the mother's question disrupts urgent sexual business. And we keep wondering whether this disruption is just thought-lessness due to Mrs Shandy's automatized association of cock and clock, of one of her husband's duties as *pater familias* with another, or whether she intends a critical, ironical or parodic point in interrupting him with this particular question.

This is the way of drama and theatre, which stages for us situations and dialogues the interactive dimensions of which we have largely to work out for ourselves. In drama, this applies, of course, particularly to the opening scene, in which the exposition has first to be given; in Sterne's fictions, due to the crisscrossing of stories and the discontinuous and digressive ways of narrating them, we are again and again confronted with situations where we have to find our bearings first and to establish who speaks and to what purpose. And, again as in drama and in the theatre, dialogue, spoken language and the glances and gestures accompanying it, are of the essence. The 'mini-dialogues' at the beginning of *Tristram Shandy* and *A Sentimental Journey* set the stage for numerous dialogues to follow, some of them – as the many conversations in front of the fireplace in Shandy Hall, the theological debate during the canonical dinner (IV.xxv–xxix) or Yorick's flirtatious exchanges with Madame de *** or with the beautiful Grisset (*SJ* 18–27, 51–6) – quite extended and complete with sets and everything that makes up a theatrical scene. The vividly oral and gestural quality of these dialogues constantly suggests the theatre. As Virginia Woolf acutely remarked: 'The very punctuation' – the dashes of varying lengths, the elisions, the exclamation and question marks – 'is that of speech, not writing, and brings the sound and associations of the speaking voice with it'.[12]

Even where, as so often, Sterne quite shamelessly plagiarizes sources, his rewriting gives to them a speaking voice. Here is, for instance, Robert Burton in his *Anatomy of Melancholy* on the 'Literature of Exhaustion':

> As apothecaries, we make new mixtures every day, pour out of one vessel into another; and as those old Romans robbed all the cities of the world, to set out their bad-sited Rome, we skim off the cream of other men's wits, pick the choice flowers of their tilled gardens, to set out our own sterile plots. Again, we weave the same web still, twist the same rope again and again.[13]

This is witty enough, but now listen – and I mean *listen* – to how Sterne recycles Burton's reflections on literary recycling:

> Shall we for ever make new books, as apothecaries make new mixtures, by pouring only out of one vessel into another? Are we for ever to be twisting, and untwisting the same rope? for ever in the same track–for ever at the same pace? (*TS* V.i.283)

Not only is Sterne more concise than the leisurely elaborations of Burton's prose allow for; by turning Burton's statements into questions, he gives them the rhetorical or dramatic force of speech appealing to an audience. He also tightens the parallelism of the first and the second sentence, and the patterns of repetitions he introduces – four times 'for ever', the coupling of 'twisting, and untwisting', the monosyllabic and alliterative chain of 'rope', 'track', 'pace' – enhance both the oral quality of this passage and the urgency of the appeal. Where

Burton's prose is the written language of exposition, Sterne's is oral and performative.

What cannot be suggested by paralinguistic markers such as typography (italics, bold print), punctuation or patterning alone is frequently indicated by 'stage directions' concretizing the vocal inflections ('making an exclamation, but taking care to moderate his voice at the same time') or the accompanying gesture ('turning quick upon me with the most civil triumph in the world'). These stage directions are inserted by the narrator who, like a presenter, gesticulates downstage and engages in dialogues in his own turn. In our two tiny excerpts alone he addresses himself in soliloquy or, rather, interior dialogue ('Strange! quoth I, debating the matter with myself...') and responds to one of his reader's reactions ('Pray, what was your father saying?——Nothing.'). At other places he frequently also appeals to one or the other of his characters '——If thou lookest, uncle *Toby*, in search of this mote one moment longer——thou art undone' (*TS* VIII.xxiv.482), invokes some august authority as the King of France ('SIRE, it is not well done...', *SJ* 3) or some personification ('Dear sensibility', *SJ*, 116), or turns to his friend Eugenius or his beloved Jenny or Eliza ('the little picture which I have so long worn, and so often have told thee, Eliza, I would carry with me into the grave', *SJ* 3).

Thus there is dialogue on the level of the story narrated *and* on the level of the narration of the story as well, and the constant superimposition and interpenetration of these two levels create a heightened sense of dialogicity and theatricality. The effect can be quite startling, particularly when the two levels are, as it were, dramatically short-circuited. A famous example of this occurs at the very end of the moving story of Le Fever and his son, one of the longest continuous stories in *Tristram Shandy*, set off as a cameo piece of sentimental writing from the rest (VI.vi–x). Having, through vividly staged scenes of the invalid soldier's sufferings, the son's faithfulness and Toby's and Trim's sympathetic benevolence, stimulated the emotional identification of the reader to the highest degree, Tristram proceeds to narrating the last moments of the dying lieutenant:

> The blood and spirits of *Le Fever*, which were waxing cold and slow within him, and were retreating to their last citadel, the heart,– rallied back,–the film forsook his eyes for a moment,–he looked up

wistfully in my uncle *Toby's* face,–then cast a look upon his boy,——
and that *ligament,* fine as it was,–was never broken.——
Nature instantly ebb'd again,——the film returned to its place,——
the pulse fluttered——stopp'd——went on——throb'd—stopp'd
again——moved——stopp'd——shall I go on?——No. (VI.x.353–4)

The dialogue between the characters is, at this point, already
reduced to an exchange of glances, and the only voice that is
heard is that of Tristram, not only narrating what happened way
back in 1706, many years before his birth, but enacting it,
performing in the broken, hesitant rhythms of his speech the
breaking of Le Fever's eyes and the fading of his breath. There is
a note of histrionic, even melodramatic exaggeration to this
performance, and Tristram, an experienced performer with one
eye always upon his audience, immediately throws the spanner
in his sentimental works and disrupts the illusion he has been
building up, as soon as he becomes aware of this note – or
becomes aware of the audience's awareness of it. He abruptly
turns from his scene to his readers, admitting to his manipula-
tion of their emotions: 'shall I go on?' Their 'No' is the laconic
acknowledgement that enough is indeed as good as a feast and
marks at the same time, as the last link in a chain of ever shorter
phrases, the end of Le Fever. (Things are, of course, even more
subtle and complex than that, as Tristram's performance,
including the inadvertent exaggeration and the sudden awareness of it, is staged by Sterne, the performer to the second
power, who trusts that we see through it and enjoy it all.)

As the spectators in the theatre, the readers are always
present and share Tristram's, the performer's, *hic et nunc.* For
that reason alone, the frequent theatre metaphors – the topos of
fiction as theatre familiar also from Fielding's novels – are
particularly appropriate here. In *A Sentimental Journey,* for
instance, Yorick, with his one foot in Shakespeare's play,
welcomes La Fleur 'upon the stage' (*SJ* 32). In *Tristram Shandy,*
the art of David Garrick, Sterne's friend and the greatest actor of
his age, is repeatedly invoked as a model for, and a complement
to, the literary art of storytelling:

O *Garrick!* what a rich scene of this [Walter Shandy holding forth on
the *conditio humana* to Toby] would thy exquisite powers make! and
how gladly would I write such another to avail myself of thy
immortality, and secure my own behind it. (IV.vii.228–9)

Very early in the book, Tristram already defines it as 'this dramatic work' (I.x.17); after Yorick's sermon, characterized by Walter as 'dramatic' and delivered by Trim in an appropriately theatrical manner, he drops 'the curtain over this scene' (II.xix.117), and later, to give a last example, he proudly draws attention to how the characters of the SHANDY-FAMILY are 'cast or contrasted with such a dramatic felicity' that they provide ever-changing 'exquisite scenes' 'in this whimsical theatre' of ours (III.xxxix.192).

These tropes of the theatre turn the reader into a spectator and listener, and, as in the theatre, for him and for the performers it is always 'now' – the same now, as the time-gap between the writing and the reading, which normally goes with communication via written and even more so via printed texts, seems to be suspended here. What this reader/spectator attends and witnesses is primarily Tristram's act of narrating, his performance as a narrator, his writing his *parlando*. This is the *Ur-Szene* which persists throughout the book, even in those vividly recalled or recreated scenes where it remains in the background: Tristram struggling with his life and opinions and how to tell them to himself and to others.

He is thus not only an extremely self-conscious but also an extremely audience-conscious narrator, always aware of his readers, responding to their interventions, and singling out individual readers or groups, mostly gendered groups of readers (VI.xvi.360: 'There are a thousand resolutions, Sir, both in church and state, as well as in matters, Madam, of a more private concern...') to draw their attention to particular aspects of his story or devices of his narration and engage them in a dialogue. There is the famous example in I.xx, where he sends back one of his lady readers to the preceding chapter because she has failed to draw from his words the inference that his mother is not a Papist, and takes 'my fair Lady' to task for her inattentive reading – a blame that any reader will have to bear as the inference is based on an arcane 'memoire' of the theologians of the Sorbonne. Tristram continues to play such games through-out his book, enjoining his readers that 'nose' means a nose and nothing else (III.xxxi) or encouraging the gentleman reader to fill a page left empty with a portrait 'as like your mistress as you can——as unlike your wife as your conscience will let you'

(VI.xxxviii.388). Even Yorick in *A Sentimental Journey*, who is much less present as a narrator than Tristram, makes a public appeal to his readers to help him find again the caged starling he had tried to set free in Paris (*SJ* 75). In such cases, the reader becomes more than the spectator in the theatre or the audience to a performance: he becomes, as it were, part of the performance, a co-performer himself or herself. This is implied in Tristram's definition of writing as 'but a different name for conversation':

> As no one, who knows what he is about in good company, would venture to talk all;—so no author, who understands the just boundaries of decorum and good breeding, would presume to think all: The truest respect you can pay to the reader's understanding, is to halve this matter amicably, and leave him something to imagine, in his turn, as well as yourself. (II.xi.88)

Seen from Sterne's, the author's, perspective this means, of course, that he has scripted the readers' roles as much as his narrator's, that both together, plus the characters performing to each other, make up the performance that is his fiction.

The act of writing itself is frequently staged. In *A Sentimental Journey*, for instance, we actually witness Yorick writing his Preface during a spare minute in a *désobligeant* coach (*SJ* 9–13), and in *Tristram Shandy* the scene of writing surfaces constantly. Tristram even provides us again and again with the exact historical date of his writing 'this very day, in which I am now writing this book for the edification of the world;–which is *March* 9, 1759', (xviii.39), with a little genre piece of himself at his desk –

> And here am I sitting, this 12th day of August, 1766, in a purple jerkin and yellow pair of slippers, without either wig or cap on... (IX.i.502)

– or relates the *hic at nunc* of writing to the times and places he writes about. Here is a bravura performance, in which Tristram superimposes three 'here and now's, or, to put it more technically, three deictic centres, one upon the other – those of two journeys through France he is narrating, and a third French journey, during which he is writing his narration:

I am this moment walking across the market-place of *Auxerre* with my father and my uncle *Toby*, in our way back to dinner–and I am this moment also entering *Lyons* with my post-chaise broke into a thousand pieces–and I am moreover this moment in a handsome pavillion built by *Pringello*, upon the banks of the *Garonne*, which Mons. *Sligniac* has lent me, and where I now sit rhapsodizing all these affairs. (VII.xxviii.426)

Attending to Tristram's writing, we share his sense of it as an ongoing process the rules and the scope of which are not predetermined, as an improvisation like that of a comedian or a professional fool, who reacts spontaneously to audience reactions or exigences of various sorts as they arise. He does, of course, make plans and suggest an overall design for his work, but most of these plans and promises are revised later or remain unfulfilled. We never get the map of the 'four or five miles' around Shandy Hall although it is already 'in the hands of the engraver': Tristram, after all, never reaches the twentieth volume of his work, where it should appear in the appendix (I.xiii.31). Nor do we get the promised two volumes per year (I.xiv.33), which might easily run into forty volumes, as between the third and fourth instalment already 'DEATH himself knocked at my door' (VII.i.395). Loose ends abound everywhere and unexpected things intrude at any time. We never get the account of his 'travels through *Denmark* with Mr. *Noddy*'s eldest son' (I.xi.22), and of the many chapters repeatedly promised – chapters on wishes or whiskers, on knots or noses, on the right and the wrong end of a woman – we only get a part. But, as if to defeat the expectation that what is envisaged is never realized, we do get a chapter on chapters immediately after it is promised (IV.ix–x.230–32) and the story of Uncle Toby's amours, announced so often that we despair of ever getting it, does, in the end, provide the final climax as 'the choicest morsel of what I have to offer to the world' (IX.xxiv.527).

The narrator as *improvvisatore* 'never blot[s] anything out' (VII.xxvi.422) – how could he possibly, as the show or the writing goes on and on? Nor does he plan the order of his text but relies upon the moment's intuition – or, mock-heroically, upon divine inspiration – for stringing his sentences, paragraphs, chapters, and books together: 'I begin with writing the first sentence—— and trusting to Almighty God for the second' (VIII.ii.450). Like any live performance, his is alive to changing circumstances and unforeseen, even unforeseeable interventions and exigences: 'much unexpected business [may] fall out betwixt the reader and myself, which may require immediate dispatch' (I.xiii.31). Where the contemporary novel – Richardson in particular – strove towards more tightly knit teleological plots based on the plausibility and predictability of events and thus tried to liberate the genre from the haphazardness of romance and the picaresque, Tristram prides himself on his ability to constantly defeat his reader's expectations:

> What these perplexities of my uncle *Toby* were,——'tis impossible for you to guess;–if you could,–I should blush; not as a relation,–not as a man,–nor even as a woman,–but as an author; insomuch as I set no small store by myself on this very account, that my reader has never been able to guess at anything. And in this, Sir, I am of so nice and singular a humour, that if I thought you was able to form the least judgement or probable conjecture to yourself, of what was to come in the next page,–I would tear it out of my book. (I.xxv.64)

Such a performance cannot have a proper ending: its open-endedness is a necessary part of its performative logic: 'It must follow, an' please your worships, that the more I write, the more I shall have to write – and consequently, the more your worships read, the more your worships will have to read' (IV.xiii.234). No wonder then, that both *Tristram Shandy* and *A Sentimental Journey* do not only contain many fragments, but remain fragments in themselves. They are not just incomplete because Death finally took the pen out of Sterne's hands (which, of course, he did); they are fragments as an art form *sui generis* and are, as such, paradoxically incomplete and finished at the same time. In this, they can be seen as anticipations of the Romantic aesthetics of the fragment and demonstrate already the fascination of Romantic ironists with the infinite – an infinite which can only be represented in the unfinished.[14]

In the final analysis, Sterne's texts are performative in the sense that they enact what they speak about. They already fulfil what Thomas Mann aimed at in his own fiction: 'always and consistently to be that of which it speaks'.[15] This is most evident with reference to principles of textualization. For instance, Sterne's texts do not only digress frequently, so frequently that the distinction between the main theme and the digression is in constant danger of collapsing altogether; they also frequently speak about and thematize digression: how digressions paradoxically contribute to the progressive movement of his narrative machinery and how they are the sunshine, the life, the soul of reading (I.xxii). Of course, in such talk about digressions Tristram actually digresses, and in a last variation on this paradox, this autoreferential loop, he goes one step further and makes it explicit: 'in talking of my digression ——I declare before heaven I have made it!' (IX.xv.518). Another repeatedly employed device of his is the rhetorical figure of *aposiopesis*, indicated by dashes or asterisks. Again, he does not only use it but comments upon it and its uses, and again in one instance he short-circuits using and mentioning it by defining it through producing an instance of it:

> 'My sister, mayhap, quoth my uncle *Toby*, does not choose to let a man come so near her****.' Make this dash,——'tis an Aposiopesis.– Take that dash away, and write Backside,–'tis Bawdy.–Scratch Backside out, and put *Cover'd-way* in,–'tis a Metaphor (II.vi.81)

And similarly, in the passage about plagiarism quoted above, where Tristram laments the mere recycling of older texts, having just decided to break with this lamentable custom of literary borrowing and theft by throwing the key to his library into a deep well, he actually plagiarizes Burton's *Anatomy of Melancholy*, a book, moreover, that famously instances here as everywhere the all-pervasiveness of an acknowledged and unacknowledged dependence on 'the *relicks of learning*' (V.i. 283).

Generalizing from here, one can argue that Sterne's fictions constantly enact and perform what they speak about. They even open up little showcases which exhibit miniature models of how they are made and what they are about.[16] André Gide, himself a master of this device, has used the heraldic metaphor of *mise en abîme* to characterize the form and function of such embedded texts or elements of texts which illuminate by way of correspondence and contrast certain features of the embedding larger text. In *A Sentimental Journey*, for instance, we find embedded within the fragmentary travelogue two fragments explicitly highlighted as such through their chapter-headings 'A' or 'The Fragment' (*SJ* 34–5, 101–7). Both define the particular kind of fragment that *A Sentimental Journey* is primarily by way of contrast: they are fragments in a philological sense, the fragmentary remains of a text that has not survived in its entirety, be it, as in the first case, the few extant verses of a hymn to Cupid from Euripides's lost *Andromeda*, or, in the second, a few pages, used for wrapping up butter, from a (fictive) manuscript in the French of Rabelais's time. In pointed contrast, *A Sentimental Journey*, as well as *Tristram Shandy*, never existed as complete texts and their various incompletions – the abrupt breaking off *in medias res* at the end, but also the loose ends and the *lacunae* within the text, the missing chapters, the empty pages, the asterisks and the dashes – are intentional and self-conscious stagings of an incompletion that dramatizes the impossibility of ever completely rendering reality in writing and challenges and stimulates the reader's imaginative coopera-tion.[17] No *force majeure* has destroyed or prevented their wholeness; they rather sacrifice the appearance of being whole and complete to 'the great saint Paraleipomenon' (*TS* III.xxx-vi.184), the patron saint of all that is omitted or discarded.

Such fragments *mise en abîme* abound in *Tristram Shandy*, the most spectacular being 'The story of the king of *Bohemia* and his seven castles' in VIII.xix, which, in spite of Trim's six brave attempts to tell it, never gets beyond the first sentence. In this, it mirrors Tristram's attempts to tell the story of his own life, which never gets beyond the first phase of being conceived, born, baptized and put into trousers. His narrative dilemmas and aporias as well as the solutions to them he experiments with, find, however, wider mirrors in the hobbyhorses of his uncle and his father. Sterne himself in one of his letters has already linked writing to riding a hobbyhorse: 'I shall write as long as I live, 'tis, in fact, my hobby-horse' (*L* 143). And in *Tristram Shandy* the equestrian metaphor of writing as riding[18] links the narrator's attempts of writing his life and opinions to Walter's and Toby's hobbyhorsical projects.

The riding trope per se enacts both the physical energy that goes into the writing and the breathless speed of it: 'What a rate I have gone on at, curvetting and frisking it away, two up and two down for four volumes together' – and so on for the whole chapter IV.xx, not looking back once at the 'scaffolding of the undertaking criticks' he has broken through in full gallop nor at the bishop he has splashed (IV.xx.245). In travel writing, this metaphor is given back its literal meaning, as Tristram, riding through France and writing France in volume VII, distinguishes between travel writers who *'wrote and gallop'd'*, those who *'gallop'd and wrote'* and finally those who 'have *wrote-galloping,* which is the way I do at present' (VII.iv.398).

Riding a *hobby*-horse, of course, adds further, particular connotations. As a hobbyhorse is, in its immediate sense, a children's toy, riding one exposes its rider to the ridicule of infantilism and eccentricity. Uncle Toby's hobbyhorse – fortifications and his wargames on the bowling green – is of 'great singularity' (I.xiv.62), not unlike Don Quixote's Rosinante or, if it comes to that, Yorick's sorry jade. Riding a hobbyhorse is less a matter of energy and speed directed towards some predetermined destination; hobbyhorses have an inclination rather to amble or race at their own will and in their own direction. Their impetus, their momentum, is beyond the rider's complete control, and the hobbyhorse is, therefore, an apt metaphor for Tristram's ambling and rambling ways of telling his story as well as for the aimless wandering of the sentimental traveller Yorick, who drifts with every current of whim and chance, 'interests his heart in everything' and has 'eyes to see, what time and chance are perpetually holding out to him as he journeyeth on his way' (*SJ* 28).

There are, however, also 'dark strokes in the HOBBY-HORSE' (*TS* I.ix.15), there is a darker, pathological strain to riding a hobbyhorse – the danger of being ridden by it, the danger of obsessive monomania. This darker strain casts its shadow across Sterne's 'amiable humorists' (S. M. Tave)[19] and puts limits to their amiability, and it also casts its shadow across the metafictional metaphor of writing as riding. Walter Shandy's systems and theories of names and noses, of obstetrics, economics and auxiliary verbs are vivid reflector images not only of Tristram's exhilaratingly eccentric narrative ways and means, but also of their self-defeating counter-productiveness. In this sense, Walter writing his 'TRISTRA-*paedia*' (V.xvi), expecting to bring whatever he has to say on the government of childhood and adolescence into the small compass of a duodecimo volume, yet never getting anywhere near finishing his ever growing *summa paedagogica*, is a performance that pre-enacts, as it were, some of the major dilemmas of Tristram's project of writing his own Tristrapaedia, i.e. his 'Life and Opinions'. Tristram's autobiographical dilemma, namely that the writing of his life takes up more time than the life itself and that therefore 'the more I write, the more I shall have to write' (IV.xiii.234), finds an exact, if reversed mirror-image in Walter's dilemma. The more Walter writes, the wider grows the gap between his writing and the life – Tristram's life – his writing is supposed to govern:

> he was three years and something more, indefatigably at work, and at last, had scarce completed, by his own reckoning, one half of his undertaking: the misfortune was, that I was all that time totally neglected and abandoned to my mother [...]. (V.xvi.309)

The more Walter writes, the more superfluous, even counter-productive does his writing become and the more evident is also the vanity of such striving for encyclopaedic completeness.

A similar paradox or aporia is dramatized in Uncle Toby's hobbyhorse, which begins as an attempt to narrate as clearly and completely as possible the traumatic story of how he was wounded in the groin during the Siege of Namur: the frustrations of telling his story by verbal means alone lead him to engage the help of two-dimensional visual models, of maps and ballistic charts, and finally of the ever more detailed and concrete three-dimensional models, the miniature fortifications, with which he and Trim replay the sieges on the bowling-green of Shandy Hall. From language to visual image to performances *en miniature*: this trajectory points towards a complete and full-scale repetition of the traumatic scene, where representation and reality would coincide, as its ideal vanishing point. This is, of course, unattainable – as unattainable for Uncle Toby as it is for Tristram, the literary narrator of his own variously wounded life, ingeniously and desperately as he may try to render it in its entirety and to re-enact it in its performative concreteness.

Moreover, the increasing concreteness and completeness of Toby's representations does not really solve his problem of communication, which first made him embark upon this trajectory. He rather loses sight of his initial aim to communicate to others where and how exactly he was wounded. The models he employs develop their own momentum, and he ends up in solipsistic games which he only shares with Trim. This is a danger that looms over Tristram's idiosyncratic ways of telling his own story as well, and of which he is constantly aware – the danger of losing himself in his hobbyhorsical performances and, by doing so, losing his audience for them. There is hope, however, for both of them. Toby may not break through the barrier of communication in his move from language and maps to performances, but it helps him to regain his health. His wound, so ominously related to impotence, begins to heal once he moves from the town to the country and from verbal narration to performative games. And similarly, Tristram's and Sterne's narrative performances may not solve the problems of language and communication, yet they are conducive to health, a cure to both writer and reader. As Tristram has it in one of his declarations of intent for his book, characteristically couched in elaborate physiological terms:

> If 'tis wrote against any thing,——'tis wrote, an' please your worships, against the spleen; in order, by a more frequent and more convulsive elevation and depression of the diaphragm, and the succussations of the intercostal and abdominal muscles in laughter, to drive the *gall* and other *bitter juices* from the gall bladder, liver, and sweet-bread of his majesty's subjects, with all the inimicitious passions which belong to them, down into their duodenums. (IV.xxii.247)

This, of course, distinguishes Tristram's hobbyhorse, his writing, from the hobbyhorses his father and his uncle ride: it is ridiculous as theirs – but he knows it is ridiculous and wants it to be so.

4

A Cock and Bull Story

Tristram Shandy is a brick of a book nowadays, even if its original components, the nine volumes in five instalments, were quite slim, as slim as the two volumes of *A Sentimental Journey* to follow it. Sterne expressly proposed to Robert Dodsley, his first London publisher, 'a *lean* edition, in two *small* volumes, of the size of Rasselas' (L 80; my italics), i.e. Johnson's moral tale of *Rasselas, Prince of Abissinia*, which had appeared the year before *Tristram Shandy* I/II in two *octavo* volumes under the Dodsley imprint. Considered as a material object, there is thus an inbuilt tension in *Tristram Shandy* between bulk and elegant slimness, between lightness and weighty *gravitas*.[1] In its bulky entirety it is like one of those mighty tomes in which Early Modern learning shored up its encyclopaedic knowledge for posterity; in the lightweight leanness of its instalments it suggests the fleeting ephemerality of the products of a rapidly expanding market for printed matter, of theatrical improvisation, even of conversation. Its figure then is the flourish that Corporal Trim makes with his stick, asserting man's freedom, and that Tristram draws for us as an elegant arabesque (IX.iv.506).

This tension between bulk and lightness, between the learned tome and the slim volumes, can be seen as related to a tension that holds Sterne's writing in suspension throughout – the tension between scripturality and orality. His writing foregrounds and dramatizes both its own written, printed textuality and, as we have seen, its aspirations towards the spoken speech of dialogue and conversation. We listen to a voice and we read a book at one and the same time. The games Sterne constantly plays with the division in volumes and chapters, with chapterization and pagination and with the whole gamut of typographical markers, with diagrams, tabulations, citations and documentations, keep us constantly alert for the book-ishness of the book we are reading. The volume and chapter divisions that often seem to cut across the text quite arbitrarily; the missing (IV.xxiii–v.248–60) or displaced chapters and pages (IX.xviii–xix.521–2/531–3); the chapters begun more than once (e.g. VI.xxxiii–iv.383); the empty (VI.xxxviii.389), the marbled (III.xxxvi.185–6) or the black pages (I.xii.29–30); the many lacunae, 'chasms' and blanks; the documents set with original and translation facing each other (III.xi.140–47; IV.200–7); the peppering of the page with dashes and rows of asterisks of varying length ...: these are all devices and effects drawing upon the materiality and the conventions of writing, typography, printing and book-making and keep the reader constantly aware that what he or she is holding in the hand is a book made up of covers, sheets, pages and graphic markers on white paper. Even the effect of orality, of a live voice, is largely created through typographical means, through capitalization and different typefaces and through a punctuation that in its excesses and idiosyncracies again and again draws attention to itself. Sterne's and Tristram's performance is both typographical and thea-trical, and both are performance artists of graphic signs as well as of the voice and the body. 'Sterne the showman', as one of the acutest students of Sternian performative typography and visual imagery has argued, indeed 'conducts his writing like a dramatic performance wherein he can paste up drawings and emblems as accessories to his narrative.'[2]

Let us, therefore, as a first step, try to give a skeleton outline of how Sterne distributed his major narrative material across the nine volumes in five instalments. Such a tabulation is, of course, bound to be hugely, if not hilariously, reductive, unless one let it run into so many pages that it would become useless as a survey and would, actually, re-enact the aporia of Toby's, Walter's and Tristram's models and representations striving towards com-pleteness. And, to be sure, the deletion of Tristram's dramati-cally presented narrative discourse, which such a focus on the story or stories necessarily entails, is even more of a *reductio ad absurdum*: *Tristram Shandy* without Tristram struggling with the telling of his tale is, after all, almost the proverbial *Hamlet* without the Prince of Denmark.[3] Still, there are lessons to be learnt on the overall organization of Sterne's book even from so Shandean an exercise as this.

In the following tabulation, we mark the main story-line in bold letters and indent constituent events, flashbacks and flashforwards, or motifs going off at the main tangent; extended insets, i.e. texts within the text, are capitalized and the right-hand column provides a rough chronology of the narrated events.

I/II (December 1759)

Volume I

Tristram's Conception (i–iv)	1718
Tristram's Birth (v–xxi)	1718
the midwife (vii–xiii, xvii–xviii)	
Yorick and his death (x–xii)	1748
THE MARRIAGE SETTLEMENT (xic–xv)	
brother Bobby's death (xvi)	1719
Walter's theories of names (xix)	
SORBONNE MEMOIRE on baptism in utero (xx)	
labour starting (xxi)	1718
Toby's Wound and Hobbyhorse (xxi; xxiii–xxv)	1695–

Volume II

Toby's Wound and Hobbyhorse cont. (i–v)	
Tristram's Birth cont. (vi–xix)	1718
Slop called and arriving (vi–x)	
Conversation between Walter, Toby,	
Slop, Trim (xii–xix)	
Toby and Stevinus	
Toby and the fly (xii)	1728
Trim reading YORICK'S SERMON (xv–xvii)	
Slop's bag and obstetrics (xix)	

III/IV (January 1761)

Volume III

Tristram's Birth cont.	1718
Conversation between Walter, Toby, Slop, Trim cont.	
Slop's bag cont. (vii–xii)	
ERNULPHUS' CURSE (xi)	
AUTHOR'S PREFACE (xx)	
Tristram's nose broken in birth, Slop	

Tristram's Grand Tour and Maria (xxiv)	1765/6
Toby's wound (xxvi–xxviii)	1695
the cock and bull story (xxxiii)	1713

There are a number of things to be gathered at one glance from this tabulation. One is, that the initially intended and promised periodicity of 'writing and publishing two volumes of my life every year' (*TS* I.xiv.33; cf. also IV.xiii.235) obviously did not work out. Only the first three instalments follow this scheme. Then, however, it took Sterne three years to produce the next – among it volume VII which, with its apparently extraneous material, might be regarded as padding – and two more years for the last, consisting of volume IX alone.[4] This does not really mean that 'the mine of invention was exhausting itself'[5] – after all, the last three volumes are not less inventive than the previous six. It rather enacts the increasingly paradoxical complexity of his project – the more he has told us, the more he has to tell us, as everything told entails its own prehistory and its own consequences that also need to be told – and the increasingly difficult circumstances of his performance, ill health and the ever more threatening imminence of death. Volume VII occupies a crucial position here: adult Tristram's breathless flight across France, pursued by Death, dramatizes his and his creator's plight as that of another Scheherazade fending off death by telling stories, narrating quite literally for his life. And this volume, for once, has a happy ending, with Tristram out-dancing Death in a 'Gascoigne roundelay' with Nannette, gathering strength for the volumes to follow in its 'VIVA LA JOIA! FIDON LA TRISTESSA!' (VII.xliii.445).

The tabulation also shows that *Tristram Shandy* is not altogether in the hands of the great god 'Muddle', as E. M. Forster has suggested,[6] nor is it, in the words of Horace Walpole, entirely given over to the droll humour of the 'whole narration always going backwards' (*CH* 55). There is an overall shift of focus, which gives shape to the whole book: a shift from the focus upon Tristram's conception, birth and infancy in the first six volumes to that upon Uncle Toby's amours in the remaining volumes after the watershed volume VII. Moreover, this shift of focus does not come as a complete surprise but is prepared for by Tristram's repeated promises that 'uncle *Toby's* amours with widow

Wadman' (III.xxiii.168) will be 'the choicest morsel of [his] whole story' (IV.xxxii.277), and by the end of volume VI, which first faces it squarely and thus builds a bridge across the travelogue volume VII towards the remaining two volumes at long last dedicated to Toby's and Widow Wadman's erotic warfare.

To be sure, these three great narrative blocks – I–VI centred round events between 1718 and 1723, VII set in the 1760s, VIII–IX between 1701 and 1713 – do not move progressively forwards in an orderly fashion, but leap forwards and then backwards again, so far backwards indeed that, in a way, the book paradoxically ends before it begins. Within these major blocks there is, however, a discernible progression: from conception to the end of infancy, from northern England to the South of France, from actual to enacted to erotic warfare. And even if these larger movements are constantly interrupted and disrupted by flashbacks and flashforwards, by digressions and metafictional intrusions of the narrator, the reader never loses sight of them completely. We can, therefore, quite agree with Tristram when he praises the ingenious 'contrivance of the machinery of [his] work' which makes it 'digressive, and [...] progressive too – and at the same time' (I.xxii.58).

In this respect, Sterne is not unlike one of the virtuoso performers of music, singers or instrumentalists, who became so famous in his own time for their inventive ornamentation, their brilliant coloratura and cadences, their extempore variations and divisions upon given themes: elaborate as these improvisations were, at their best they never lost sight of the main musical themes, round which they played and to which they returned. After all, Sterne was a competent, maybe even an accomplished viola da gambist himself, dedicated to an instrument that was considered as *the* instrument of virtuosity and used for 'embroidering a bass with brilliant runs, arpeggios, and other embellishments' and for building up 'a polyphonic structure out of its own resources'.[7] It may be helpful, therefore, to think of Sterne's literary performances in terms of the musical practices of his age, in particular virtuoso improvisation and the 'free forms' so popular in his time, the capriccio, the prelude and the fantasia. Sterne himself certainly did – at least he has Yorick annotate his dramatic sermons with musical terms like *moderato, con strepito* or *alla capella* (VI.xi.355) and has Tristram fiddle a whole chapter as a kind of *musikalischer Scherz* (V.xv.306–7), not to mention the many variations Uncle Toby runs upon his 'Lillabullero' whistle. And when Tristram, at the end of volume VI, tries to represent his narrative procedures in a diagram, the convoluted loops and angles playing round a 'straight line', the 'line of GRAVITATION', which he constantly deviates from but never loses sight of, does resemble nothing more than musical notation (VI.xl.391–2).

Tristram's performance, like that of any virtuoso musician, relies on the mutually dependent principles of repetition and variation, of balanced parallelism and contrastive counterpoint, of a recognizable frame of order and free improvisation, of fulfilled expectations and surprising turns. Thus, for instance, the reader learns to expect one or two major insets or texts within the text of each volume, and his or her expectations, raised by the Sorbonne memoire on baptism in utero (I) and Yorick's sermon (II) are, in one way or another, fulfilled in all the following volumes, particularly impressively in Ernulphus's curse (III), Slawkenbergius's tale (IV), the fragment upon La Fousseuse and whiskers (V), the story of Le Fever (VI) and that of the Abbess of Andoüillets (VII). These insets are, however, of a hugely various nature. They range from the learned wit of mock-theological satire (I/III) to serious sermon (II), from racy fabliau (IV/V/VII) to sentimental tale (VI). Their position within each volume also varies, and so does their relation to the main Shandean plots. Finally, the insets in the last two volumes are in such a minor key that they remind the reader of the convention rather than fulfil it: the tale of the King of Bohemia (VIII) hardly gets beyond the first sentence, upon which are played ever new variations, and the invocation to the spirit of long-suffering Cervantes (IX), though beginning in the grandest of styles, is abruptly cut short after a few lines only by Tristram's recollections of his own hardships suffered during his Grand Tour of France and Italy.

Equally, the division into instalments, volumes and chapters, which suggests a firm compositional framework for Tristram's performance, works out as much as an element of surprising irregularity as of order, an element of lively rhythmic variation rather than measured equivalence. The chapters run from a few lines (e.g. IV.v.227; IX.ix.512) to many pages; the volumes, although at first sight rather similar, actually vary in length from

216 pages (IV) to 148 (IX) in their original editions, with a general *decrescendo* from the first four to the last five volumes; the instalments, finally, shrink from the longest, III/IV, with 416 pages, to the single volume IX of hardly more than a third of that. Moreover, and more importantly, these divisions very rarely function, as one would expect, as caesuras or halting places. More often than not they do *not* mark phases in the narrative or changes of scene or theme and thus their conventional closural function is highlighted by being disregarded rather than fulfilled. The narrative voice constantly plays against their beat, opening, for instance, volume III, the first of the second instalment, in the middle of a conversation which was originally begun towards the end of the first instalment – as if, for the original readers, there had not passed a year! 'I wish [...] you had seen what prodigious armies we had in Flanders', says Uncle Toby to Dr Slop at the end of chapter xviii (p. 116) in volume II, his one-track mind once again famously taking him off at a tangent from obstetrics to warfare. And the same tangential remark then opens not only the first chapter of the next volume and instalment, but also its second and sixth chapter (III.i.129; ii.130; vi.134), the repetition thus underlining for once the chapter division. Again, a musical term suggests itself for such effects, which rely on measured equivalence and play against it at the same time: syncopation, with its energizing tension between beat and rhythm, which finds its literary analogue here in the tension between the orderly segmentation into chapters and volumes on the one hand and the vagaries of the story and the performative energies of the narrative voice on the other.

Also cutting across the external divisions of instalments, volumes and chapters, as well as across the various separable story-lines, there is another constructional principle that gives shape to the apparent muddle and for which again I would like to suggest musical analogies: *tema con variazioni* and leitmotifs. There are, for instance, as we have seen, hobbyhorses – Toby's, Walter's, Tristram's – that reflect upon each other as variations upon one theme. But there are not only metaphorical and metafictional hobbyhorses and mythological Pegasuses; there are also real horses running like a leitmotif through the book: Yorick's 'lean, sorry, jack-ass of a horse', 'full brother to

Rosinante', which the horse-proud parson had eventually adopted, sacrificing his passion for elegant, full-mettled steeds to his Christian charity (I.x.19), or servant Obadiah's 'strong monster of a coach-horse', the approach of which makes Dr Slop tumble into the dirt from his own 'little diminuitive pony' (II.ix.85), to mention only the most conspicuous ones. And, no longer fully pertaining to the equine species, there are mules, the sterile offsprings of a male ass and a mare: Don Diego's mule in Slawkenbergius's tale (IV), Tristram's mule which carries him across France, and the mule that pulls the cart of the nuns of Andoüillets (VII). Beyond that are, of course, thoroughbred asses as well, both metaphorical and literal ones: the asses for which Tristram takes his reviewers (VI.i.339), the ass for which Walter decries his body in its self-willed concupiscence (VIII.xxxi.487–8) and, not to forget, the asses that are actually arses; the 'real' asses whose tails Dr Kunastrokius loves to comb with such hobbyhorsical abandon (I.vii.13) and the ass with whom Tristram communes so thoughtfully on his way from Lyons to Avignon (VII.xxxii.431–3). And from horses, mules and asses there is only a small zoological leap to other domestic quadrupeds – most notably Walter's bull, whose dubious potency provides a fitting *cadenza* to this leitmotif running through the whole cock and bull story (IX.xxxiii.542–3). Walter's bull clearly strikes an echoing note to Yorick's sorry jade, the way variations on a musical theme or leitmotifs do: both horse and bull are intended by their owners to provide a service to the parish, in both cases this service is related to procreation – the horse to send for the midwife, the bull to inseminate cows – and again, in both cases the result is far from satisfactory.

It would take a volume longer than the longest volume of *Tristram Shandy* – and much less amusing to read – to unravel all the twists and ramifications given to this one particular leitmotif and to demonstrate exhaustively how its various inflections cast ever new light upon central themes of the book, i.e. fertility and impotence, body and soul, moral will and the weaknesses of the flesh, altruism and egotism, hobbyhorses, ruling passions, sentiments, the pitfalls of communication... And, after all, the quadrupeds are just one example for such leitmotifs, picked out here at random or, perhaps, for their conspicuous size. There are many others, down to holes, bridges, machines, whiskers, knots and other odds and ends, or, on a more abstract level, travelling and warfare or gravity and falling. And it would take a volume longer than *Tristram Shandy*'s nine volumes together to identify all of them and elaborate upon their contribution to the thematic progression of the book and upon how they interrelate one with the other. Together, these leitmotifs crisscrossing each other give a symphonic and contrapuntal structure to the book. Or, to change my metaphor, they weave a net or tapestry that holds it together across its division into chapters and volumes and its various narratives. The emphasis here is, of course, on the weaving rather than the tapestry: not on the finished, spatialized product but on the process in time, the narrator's performance and the reader's re-enactment of it.

Variations upon a theme involve both repetition and contrast, both likeness and difference. As Tristram, in his 'Author's Preface' (III.xx), argues against the great Locke, one needs judgement as well as wit, the judgement to separate from each other ideas wherein can be found the least difference as well as the wit to discover resemblance or sameness in things and ideas apparently different. Again and again characters and situations are made to mirror each other to demonstrate the performer's, and to stimulate the reader's, wit and judgement. There has, as Tristram insists, never been a family as the 'SHANDY-FAMILY', 'where the characters of it were cast or contrasted with so dramatic a felicity' (III.xxxix.192). Thus, for instance, all the male members of the Shandy family show 'strong lines [...] of a family-likeness', as Tristram insists: they all demonstrate 'eccentricity' and 'an original character throughout'. At once we are confronted with two pairs of oppositions: the eccentric and odd male Shandeans vs. the Shandean females that have 'no character at all', and, as great-aunt Dinah, by marrying a coachman, is an exception to this rule, her vs. the rest of the Shandy women (I.xxi.53). Moreover, the family-likeness between the male Shandeans is insisted upon to highlight difference, 'the contrariety of humours betwixt my father and my uncle' only a few pages later (I.xxi.56). There may be only one way of being normal, but there are certainly many ways of being odd and eccentric, and Walter's and Toby's are direct opposites. Their hobbyhorses run away with them in opposite directions, their trains or chains of ideas or associations lead them off at a tangent in diametrically different directions. Toby's humour is a one-track mind, his hobbyhorse is single and simple: there is nothing in this world that he would not relate to warfare and the science of fortifications. His brother's ruling passion, in contrast, is more complex and varied; his hobbyhorse is systems and theories in general and, as he has got a different theory for each and everything, his hobbyhorse takes him everywhere. Toby's hobbyhorse, therefore, soon becomes a running gag, foreseeable in its mechanical repetitiveness, whereas Walter's ingenious theories, and the ingenious ways in which he proves them against all odds, never cease to surprise us.[8]

There are further contrasts in characterization that are being insisted upon again and again. There is, for instance, the contrast between the eloquent and the laconic. Mrs Shandy and Toby are the silent ones: although hers is the first reported speech in the book ('Pray, my dear, have you not forgot to wind up the clock'), Mrs Shandy, to her husband's aggravation, hardly says anything or merely repeats what he has just said (e.g. VI.xviii); Toby, unless elaborating upon military lore, is rather tongue-tied and prefers whistling 'Lillabullero' to ventilating his feelings. And the two eloquent ones, Walter and Trim, differ as much as they are alike in their eloquence: Walter's is the eloquence of a self-taught scholar spreading his rhetorical and dialectical feathers, Latinate in diction and fraught with classical or curious learning; Trim's, in contrast, has a vernacular zest and is an eloquence of the body as much as of words. One of a number of situations in which this contrast is driven home occurs when the news of the death of Bobby – Tristram's brother – reaches Shandy Hall (V.ii–xvi). Where the father rises rhetorically and philosophically to the occasion and embarks upon a long oration on the vanity of death and its horrors and on Socrates's heroic defiance of it, completely losing sight of poor Bobby, Trim, the uncle's servant, simply speaking his sorrow – 'I lament for him from my heart and soul' – and enacting the boy's sudden death by dropping his hat upon the ground (V.vii.297–8), moves everybody to tears.

This contrast between different kinds of eloquence and different types of rhetoricians, which runs through the whole book as another theme with variations, is explicitly and proudly drawn attention to by narrating Tristram. He sets up 'Corporal

Trim and my father, two orators so contrasted by nature and education, haranguing over the same bier', as just one example for a wider and also recurrently staged contrast – that between the gentry and their retainers, between parlour and kitchen. And just as the pointed juxtaposition of Walter's and Toby's speeches 'over the same bier' reminds one of similarly contrasted funeral orations of Brutus and Mark Antony in Shakespeare's *Julius Caesar* (III.ii), the wider, class-bound contrast suggests the parallelism of major and minor plots in his romantic comedies, brought down to the level of a bourgeois rather than aristocratic society. The Shandy family, although 'a simple machine', is constructed in a way

> that whatever motion, debate, harangue, dialogue, project, or dissertation, was going forwards in the parlour, there was generally another at the same time, and upon the same subject, running parallel along with it in the kitchen. (V.vi.295)

Trim's wooing of Bridget in volume IX, running parallel along with his master's amours with her mistress, widow Wadman, is but the concluding and crowning instance of this constructional principle.

Setting up such and many other insistently reiterated analogies between characters, between situations, between themes, Tristram turns his narration into a veritable hall of mirrors or chamber of echos. The window sash that falls on young Tristram's penis in V.xvii echoes the fall of the hot chestnut into the unnamable aperture of Phutatorius's breeches (IV.xxvii), which is, in its turn, an echo of the fall of the piece of stone from the parapet of a horn-work that mangled Toby's groin at the siege of Namur (I.xxi). And all three of them are analogous as events governed by the laws of gravity and ballistics and – on a mythological scale – are distant yet distinct analogies to the biblical story of the aboriginal Fall in that they all connect falling in one way or another with sexual parts.[9] However, as Walter Shandy knows, analogies always involve difference: 'ANALOGY, replied my father, is the certain relation and agreement, which different——' (II.vii.83). The abortive definition, characteristically interrupted by a rap at the door, breaks off on a note of difference; cocksure certainty is cut short at the point where the different and differentiation are introduced.

In these continued games of identity, likeness and difference, all fixed notions and concepts become slippery – down to the right and the wrong end of a woman (II.vii.82, and again IX.iii.505), the question which first occasioned Walter's attempt at defining 'analogy'. The conjunctions of likeness and the divisions of difference extend beyond characters, situations and leitmotifs into language itself, cutting right through individual words. 'A rose is a rose is a rose': maybe for Gertrude Stein, but certainly not for Sterne. As much as Tristram insists that a nose is a nose is a nose, Sterne demonstrates that this is patently untrue. It is, paradoxically, this very insistence –

> For by the word *Nose*, throughout all this long chapter of noses and in every other part of my work, where the word *Nose* occurs,–I declare, by that word I mean a Nose, and nothing more or less.

– which stimulates the awareness that here as elsewhere there are always at least 'two senses' at stake, 'a dirty and a clean one', as Eugenius points out. And, as Tristram has to concede, even an explicit definition is no way out here, as 'to define–is to distrust' and involves the acknowledgement of the existence and intrusiveness of the very meanings the definition is intended to rule out. (III.xxxi.178)

Where Gertrude Stein's famous tautology provocatively disregards the relationship between words and things by insisting that the only true definition of a word is the word itself and that the thing is nothing else but the thing itself, the semantic games, experiments and speculations in *Tristram Shandy* revolve around this very axis. In Tristram's view there are things, words and the users of words, and as these three belong to different orders of being, their relationship is a precarious and slippery one.

To achieve order and stability here, the Royal Society in the second half of the seventeenth century had already tried to impose a linguistic regimen that would allow one word, and one word only, for each thing, thus establishing a rigorously univocal relationship between words and things in which then the thing itself would ideally replace the word. Two generations later, Swift, Sterne's Anglican confrère, was to expose such semantic naivety to general ridicule: in the third book of *Gulliver's Travels* he has the scientists of his Lagado 'Academy of

Inventors' communicate not by means of words and verbal language but – not unlike Toby and his three-dimensional models – by showing to each other the things themselves, which they carry around with them in huge bags – the most obvious problem here being, of course, that these bags would have to be big enough to contain the whole world.

Before Swift's satire, John Locke had already addressed himself to the problem of words and their reference in all philosophical seriousness. Book III of *An Essay Concerning Human Understanding* (1690; 5th edn 1706), 'Of Words', is entirely dedicated to it. As an empirical philosopher, he has to deny himself any recourse to a 'natural' relationship between words and things as well as to any transcendental signifier that would authorize their meanings: for him, words are arbitrary signs which we use 'for the recording of our own thoughts' and 'for the communication of our thoughts to others', and their meaning or reference is established through use and convention. This works quite well in '*civil* use', i.e. in 'common conversation and commerce about the ordinary affairs and conveniences of civil life in the society of men one amongst another'.[10] But, as he demonstrates in chapter ix, 'Of the Imperfection of Words', it leads to unresolvable problems when it comes to the '*philosophical* use' of words:

> Common use *regulates the meaning of words* pretty well for common conversation; but, nobody having an authority to establish the precise signification of words, nor determine to what *ideas* anyone shall annex them, common use is not sufficient to adjust them to philosophical discourses... (271–2)

The way out suggested by the Royal Society and its first historian, Bishop Thomas Sprat, namely authoritative and explicit definitions, leads nowhere; with words and expressions for 'complex ideas' it rather tends to aggravate the problem, as any definition requires further definitions:

> comments beget comments, and explications make new matter for explications; and of limiting, distinguishing, varying the significa-tion of these moral words, there is no end. These *ideas* of men's making are, by men still having the same power, multiplied *in infinitum*. (p. 73)

This *regressus ad infinitum* is certainly after Sterne's own heart, and it does, therefore, not come as a surprise that he has Tristram single out this very chapter of Locke's book: 'Well might *Locke* write a chapter upon the imperfections of words–' (V.vii.297). What may appear at first sight as Tristram subscribing whole-heartedly to Locke's ideas and paying his homage to the great philosopher is, however, a subtle critique. The context of Tristram's reference to Locke is maid Susannah's reaction to the news of Bobby's death: what they mean to her is a 'green sattin night-gown' to be given to her by her mistress, who will have to go into mourning. What is at stake here is – in Locke's words – surely not the philosophical, but the civil use of words; yet even here language quite obviously is a far from perfect means of communication.

Thus, things are even worse than Locke envisaged them: words and language slip through rational control in everyday situations as much as in philosophical discourse. What is an exception with Locke is the rule with Sterne, as literally hundreds of misunderstandings, double entendres, equivocations and puns throughout *Tristram Shandy* demonstrate. You may want to define words as Tristram does the nose, the button-hole and the whiskers: what you exclude in your definition becomes even more obtrusive. Or, conversely, you may split them into two, as the Abbess of Andoüillets and Sister Margarita do: *bou* plus *ger* and *fou* plus *ter* will never be semantically void and will always suggest buggery and fucking, even if their two mules do not get the message (VII.xxv.420–21). Each intended meaning has one or more shadows, and this even extends to words as innocent as *where*: 'where' on the battlefield, and 'where' in his body Toby was wounded are two crucially different matters – and the equivocation remains unresolved almost until the end of the book and is then only resolved with the help of a deictic gesture of Trim's hand (IX.xxviii.536–7).

These constant frictions and hitches in the process of verbal communication constantly foreground language as a problem and occasion ever new reflections, particularly on Tristram's part, upon the workings and the limits of language, on 'the unsteady uses of words, which have perplexed the clearest and most exalted understandings' and on how words, not ideas, have put his life in jeopardy (II.ii.71–72). The theory of semantics projected in these meta-linguistic reflections appears to anticipate Wittgenstein's concept of 'Sprachspiele' and his performative theory of meaning, in which the meaning of a word is not fixed in any dictionary nor in a stable reference to what is outside language, but resides in, coincides with, and *is* its use. In this respect, the two levels of metalinguistic and of metafictional awareness which overarch the plot, the situations and the dialogue and on which Tristram acts out his role of narrator, are not only structurally equivalent but are both concerned with language and fiction as performance.

Words being as imperfect as the language games of *Tristram Shandy* demonstrate, even more imperfect than Locke had feared, one wonders how the various members of the Shandy family manage to communicate with each other at all. And communicate they quite obviously do, even quite intensively! And this, moreover, in spite of the fact that each of them seems to be locked in his or her own private world, chained to his or her own chain or train of associations and ideas. This is, next to the imperfections of words and closely related to it, the second major point round which Sterne's dialogue with Locke revolves.[11] Locke had concluded the second book of his *Essay Concerning Human Understanding*, 'Of Ideas', with a chapter 'Of the Association of Ideas', and it is this chapter xxxiii that Sterne most insistently refers to throughout *Tristram Shandy*. Locke argues here that the ideas in our minds are not independent of each other but follow one upon the other in a chain or train. He distinguishes between two principles of concatenation:

> Some of our *ideas* have a natural correspondence and connexion one with another; it is the office and excellency of our reason to trace these, and hold them together in that union and correspondence which is founded in their peculiar beings. Besides this, there is another connexion of *ideas* wholly owing to chance or custom: *ideas* that in themselves are not at all of kin, come to be so united in some men's mind that it is very hard to separate them, they always keep in company, and the one no sooner at any time comes into the understanding but its associate appears with it; and if they are more than two which are thus united, the whole gang, always inseparable, show themselves together. (p. 219)

Again, as in his discussion of words, there is one principle that makes for rational order and another one that endangers it. In the case of words this was the difference between the consensual use of words in civic conversation on the one hand and the absence of authority over the meaning of words in philosophical discourse on the other. Here it is nature and reason that make for a rational and natural concatenation of ideas, and chance and custom that threaten to disrupt this orderly progression and run wild like a gang of criminals. This kind of *penser sauvage*, in which private and idiosyncratic associations, acquired through habit or chance coincidences go off at a tangent from reasonable argument, is for Locke the 'disease' of reason, a 'sort of madness', 'fitter for *Bedlam* than civil conversation' (pp. 218–19).

And again, Sterne's attention focuses on the second, the unruly principle. His very first narrative move in the book already bears this out: the story of how Mrs Shandy interrupted her husband's conjugal ministration by asking him whether he has not forgotten to wind up the clock. To an outside observer this question may appear to be quite beside the point; to her, however, custom and chance, i.e. the family routine of the Shandy household, have indelibly linked her husband's periodically regulated sexual activity to his other domestic duty, the winding up of the clock. Tristram, begot in a *coitus interruptus*, thus sees himself as the victim of 'an unhappy association of ideas',

> which strange combination of ideas, the sagacious *Locke*, who certainly understood the nature of these things better than most men, affirms to have produced more wry actions than all other sources of prejudice whatsoever. (I.iv.9)

The homage that Tristram pays to sagacious Locke, here as elsewere, is again relativized and put into question by the context: Mrs Shandy, although clearly instancing Locke's chain of associations based on chance or custom here, is equally clearly *not* a case for Bedlam. Nor are Walter Shandy, Uncle Toby, Dr Slop, or, if it comes to that, Tristram himself, even if their various eccentricities, idiosyncracies, and idées fixes, their various whims, oddities and hobbyhorses all qualify them for Locke's second category!

What is the deviation, the exception in Locke, again becomes the rule and norm in Sterne's world. In that, Sterne is much closer to the 'associationist' psychology of his own time, to

David Hartley, for instance, whom, however, he does not refer to, than to the celebrated philosopher of more than two generations previously, to whom he pays elaborate homage. There is also a significant difference in tone between Locke and Sterne here: where Locke castigates 'this sort of unreasonableness' (p. 218) as an intellectual vice, as a betrayal of reason that ends in madness, assembling on his way a Bedlam of increasingly dangerous perversions worth the satirical pen of a Swift or Pope, Sterne treats it with humour and sympathy. After all, this is how we all are, not just perfectly functioning reasonable beings but drifting with our whims, driven by our ruling passions and riding our hobbyhorses. Moreover, the philosopher protests too much. The very violence with which Locke rejects these 'wrong and unnatural combinations of ideas' (p. 223) and excludes them from right reason, may be seen as giving away his anxiety that the dividing line between them and a 'natural correspondence' of ideas may not be as watertight as the enlightened philosopher desperately wants it to be. This very question where and how to draw a line here, or whether it is possible to draw one at all – the question suppressed in the philosopher's text and concealed behind an over-asserted dichotomy, is allowed free play in the fictionalist's performances.

One perspective that Sterne opens up in the games he plays with Locke is that Locke's own theories of chains and trains of ideas are not altogether totally different from, say, the hobbyhorsical systems expounded by Walter Shandy and are, therefore, far from safely lodged within his own system with the entirely rational ideas that 'have a natural correspondence and connexion one with another'. After all, they are based on a metaphor, and metaphors are notoriously wilful and capricious. This becomes evident for instance, when Locke expands and elaborates upon the metaphor of chains and trains and defines custom as

> but trains of motion in the animal spirits, which, once set a-going, continue in the same steps they have been used to; which by often treading, are worn into a smooth path, and the motion in it becomes easy and, as it were, natural. (p. 219)

Here, the metaphor spawning personifications and a plot is hardly in line with Locke's own norms of right reasoning. It is 'odd' and 'extravagant' (p. 218) itself, and it takes Sterne little effort to carry it to absurd lengths – as he does, for instance, on the first page already, before he has even mentioned Locke:

> you have all, I dare say, heard of the animal spirits, as how they are transfused from father to son, &c. &c.–and a great deal to that purpose:–Well, you may take my word, that nine parts in ten of a man's sense or nonsense, his successes and miscarriages in this world depend upon their motions and activity, and the different tracks and trains you put them into; so that when they are once set a-going, whether right or wrong, 'tis not a half-penny matter,–away they go cluttering like hey-go-mad; and by treading the same steps over and over again, they presently make a road of it, as plain and as smooth as a garden-walk, which, when they are once used to, the Devil himself sometimes shall not be able to drive them off it. (I.i.5–6)

The facetiousness of tone and the homely details which concretize Locke's metaphor already make a parody of it. And when, on the next page and in the next chapter, he brings together the notion of animal spirits with that of the 'HOMUNCULUS', the spermatozoon of Early Modern medicine, which he literalizes into 'my little gentleman' (I.ii.6),[12] his sceptically amused distance to all such systems – their fantastic inventiveness, their incongruities and the incompatibilities between them – is further dramatized.

Sterne's Locke, focused upon in an uncharacteristic detail (the chapter on the association of ideas is, after all, a sideline and an afterthought to the *Essay*, not inserted before its fourth edition), parodied through exaggeration and his arguments mingled with quaint medical lore made quainter in the facetious account: this Locke is not that different from all the other providers of curious and arcane learning in the book, from a Robert Burton, for instance. This Locke is not the key to *Tristram Shandy*, as earlier scholars had it; he does not furnish the philosophical matrix on which Sterne's view of man, his ways of feeling, thinking and speaking, is based. Rather, as Traugott first pointed out, Sterne 'by developing the possibilities of confusion and absurdity in Locke's rational system has created a dramatic engine which controls situation and character'.[13]

What has Sterne to set against his Lockean worst-case scenario? Why does communication not break down completely in the face of imperfections of words permeating all language and fortuitous associations of ideas locking each individual within his or her own private world? There are two compensations he has to offer for the inadequacies of language and for the danger of solipsism, and they are closely related to each other: the language of the body for the first, and sympathy and sentiment for the second. Both attempt to bridge the chasm between *res extensa* and *res cogitans*, the material and the intellectual world, the body and the mind or soul, which rationalist philosophy since Descartes had opened up. '*Des Cartes*' actually makes a brief appearance in *Tristram Shandy* – only to have his own attempt at bridging the gap by giving the soul a material habitat in 'the *pineal* gland of the brain' and making it interact with the body through vital spirits, dismissed as another specimen of quack philosophy, one not even Walter Shandy falls for (II.xix.119).

Sterne and Tristram obviously do not believe in such a mechanical link between body and soul; for them there are half-way meeting grounds that make the body transparent to the soul. As the *Tristram Shandy* project progresses, they gain in confidence that body and soul form a psychosomatic unity, in which the body articulates the soul and the soul informs the body. At first Tristram agrees with Lucian's Momus, who had blamed the gods for having forgotten to instal a window in the human breast, which would allow one to look directly through the body into a character's soul; he therefore ingeniously suggests a character's hobbyhorse as a surrogate for the missing 'Momus's glass' (I.xxiii.59), drawing his characters from their hobbyhorses. Later on, however – and in *A Sentimental Journey*, which can do without hobbyhorses altogether, even more so than in *Tristram Shandy* – the body itself, transparent to the soul, becomes the glass that Momus had missed, or rather overlooked.

Therefore, Tristram constantly writes and reads the body language (posture, gesture, facial expression, tears, laughter, glances etc.) and the corporeal aspects of the language (voice, inflection, intonation etc.) of his characters and shows how eloquent they are of their inner life and soul, their emotions and sentiments: the painstakingly exact descriptions of Trim's attitude while he reads Yorick's sermon (II.xvii.97–9) and of the way he drops his hat at the news of Bobby's death (V.vii. 298–9), of Walter struggling to take out his handkerchief from his right pocket with his left hand (III.ii.131) or of Widow Wadman, fallen in love with Toby, kicking her folded-in nightshift open (VIII.ix.456) are only a few of the more memorable instances of this. Moreover, he frequently thematizes and theorizes the extent to which non-verbal communication makes up for the imperfections of verbal language, how and why it is more persuasive and moving, and how reliable it is as an indicator of what goes on within a person's mind. The initial scepticism on this point – 'our minds shine not through the body' (I.xxiii.60) – gradually gives way to a much more optimistic view:

> There is, continued my father, a certain mien and motion of the body and all its parts, both in acting and speaking, which argues a man *well within*; [...] There are a thousand unnoticed openings, continued my father, which let the penetrating eye at once into a man's soul [...]. (VI.v.343)

Freud quoted this very passage in his *Psychopathology of Everyday Life* (1898–1924) as a shining example of 'psychoanalytic observation having to cede priority to poets' when it comes to 'symptomatic actions'.[14] Mind you, it is the father speaking here, and that exposes this view to the suspicion that it is just another one of his eccentric hobbyhorsical systems. Tristram himself, however, also comes round to such a view and dramatizes it, albeit with much greater subtlety than his father is capable of, in a brilliant setpiece late in the book (IX.xx.523): Uncle Toby's offer to show Mrs Wadman 'the very place' where he was wounded, makes her run through the whole gamut of blushing, looking towards the door, turning pale, blushing slightly again, recovering her natural colour and blushing worse than ever. Toby, of course, lacks the 'penetrating eye' postulated by Walter and realizes nothing. Tristram, however, undertakes to 'translate' this 'for the sake of the unlearned reader' into an interior monologue, attributing in his verbal transcription to each of her facial expressions a precise nuance of meaning, from *'L—d! I cannot look at it——'* to *'——I will look at it'*. In contrast, the verbal dialogue between the two, which runs on simultaneously, does not get anywhere, be it only due to the fact that 'the very place' means entirely different things for the two – which shows once again 'what little knowledge is got by mere words–we must go up to the first springs', the first springs being, of course, the body and its desires and expressiveness.

Tristram's awareness of the eloquence of the body goes far beyond what rhetorics knew and taught about the importance of *actio*, i.e. the delivery, the performance of speech. For him, the body is eloquent even where it does not accompany speech, as, for instance, his encounters with the ass (VII.xxxii) and with mad, lovelorn Maria (IX.xxiv) demonstrate: although the one has no language beyond turning its head or looking wistfully, and the other has lost her language and expresses herself only in the melancholy cadences warbled on her pipe and – again – in wistful glances, Tristram understands them 'perfectly' (VII.xxxii.432). (Why this kind of communication, both in *Tristram Shandy* and in *A Sentimental Journey*, seems to work particularly well with asses and women will need further exploration.) Such communication beyond words is only possible as for him there is no rift between body and mind. The one is the reverse side of the other – or, as he has it in one of his quaint and homely metaphors:

> A man's body and his mind, with the utmost reverence to both I speak it, are exactly like a jerkin, and a jerkin's lining;–rumple the one–you rumple the other. (III.iv.132)

Body and mind do not meet in one particular organ, be that Descartes's pineal gland, Borri's 'cellulae of the occipital parts of the cerebrellum', or Walter's *'medulla oblongata'* (II.xix.119–20); they are closely contiguous one with the other throughout. Therefore Sterne's 'physiological writing', as I would like to call it, attends as much to the surface of the body, the skin, as to its inner organs – to the suffusion of blood in a character's vein that makes for blushes, as to the tracks of the animal spirits in the blood; as much to the facial expressions of laughter as to the workings of the spleen and the diaphragm that produce them (cf. IV.xxii). With such a psychosomatic approach, in which psychology and physiology constantly translate themselves one into the other, the mind or soul is no longer an unconditioned transcendental absolute, nor is it a stable, unchanging entity: it is, to a large extent, determined by heredity, by acquired habits and by the accidents that happen to bodies, as the fortunes of the Shandy family and those of Tristram in particular show. And it is projected and reprojected in variable spontaneous or histrionic performances of the body. In this sense, the subjectivity, i.e. the internalized sense of identity and the self-consciousness, of Sterne's characters is, indeed, 'inszenierte Subjektivität' (Wolfgang Iser).[15]

Body language or non-verbal communication as the interface between the material body and the mind is closely related to Sterne's second remedy for Rationalism and its discontents: sympathy and sentiment. As I shall discuss them more fully in the following chapter on *A Sentimental Journey*, let it suffice here to point out wherein that relationship lies. Firstly, sentiments also bridge the gap between body and mind: they are *no longer* merely bodily phenomena, although these subtle emotions of tenderness and sympathy, of wistfulness and benevolence, immediately affect the body and are affected by it in turn; and they are *not yet* intellectually conscious ideas grasped by the mind, although they are a prerequisite for them and can be raised to a fuller consciousness of themselves. And secondly: without sympathy, body language remains mute or meaningless, and what body language can communicate best of all are sentiments, not intellectual ideas. Tristram's writing of the body, and even more so Yorick's in *A Sentimental Journey*, is thus largely a writing of sentiments as states and motions of the body.

Reacting against Rationalism – or, rather, against narrow versions of Rationalism[16] – Sterne shifts the centre of gravity from the mind towards the body. Against Rationalism's flights towards pure reason, he sets his own, often comic, bathos of our natural gravitation towards the body – its more delicate states of tender sensibility as much as the bawdy of its excremental and sexual functions. Against Descartes's 'cogito ergo sum' (which he does not quote), he sets his own 'sentio ergo sum' (which he does not say in so many words, but stages in so many performances) – 'sentio' covering here the whole semantic range from sense perception to the refined and benevolent emotions privileged within a culture of Sentimentalism.

Having said all that, I hasten to add that Sterne is, of course, not an enemy of the Enlightenment: what he protests against and ridicules in his fictional performances, is a Rationalism too narrow to encompass wit as well as judgement, imagination as well as reason, and what he opposes is a Materialism for which the body is just matter and not sentient and vibrant with sentiment, and human conduct just self-seeking and incapable

73

of benevolent sympathy. Within such a wider notion of Enlightenment, of a criticism of the Enlightenment from within, Sterne's *Tristram Shandy* is an 'Essay Concerning Human Understanding' as much as Locke's. Indeed, it is even more of an 'essay' than Locke's as, 'hat[ing] set dissertations' (III.xx.162), Tristram's reasoning and arguing is much more provisional and tentative than the philosopher's and conveys much more of the sense of *penser en movement*, for which Montaigne's *Essais* – admired and repeatedly quoted in *Tristram Shandy* – have been praised.[17] And, what is more, its concern with human understanding has a wider range than Locke's.

Sterne's dialogue with Locke is so intensive because he does not only disagree with him but shares his basic empiricist assumptions: that man possesses no innate ideas, and that all the ideas that man acquires and possesses derive from two sources, sensations drawn from the experiential world and his own reflections upon them. In the words of Sterne's title: there is the lived 'Life' and there are 'Opinions'. Or, in terms of the epigraph to the first volume, taken from Epictetus's *Enchiridon*: there are the *pragmata* and the *dogmata*, the things and the opinions or notions we have of them. And there's – as Hamlet, another great sceptic, would say – the rub: as the mind has no direct access to the things but has only got sensations of them to process, the mind's notions or ideas of things are always, at *least* to a certain extent, subjective and therefore tend to proliferate and to disturb us in their proliferation. The only thing the mind can have any certain knowledge about, is its own ideas. To quote Locke's first sentence of Book IV, 'Of Knowledge and Opinion':

> Since *the mind*, in all its thoughts and reasonings, hath no other immediate object but its own *ideas*, which it alone does and can contemplate, it is evident that our knowledge is only conversant about them. (p. 191)

Tristram is, therefore, quite right when, in a dialogue with his critics, he defines Locke's *Essay* as 'a history-book, Sir, (which may possibly recommend it to the world) of what passes in a man's own mind' (II.ii.70). At the same time, however, this is one of the aptest definitions ever proffered for *Tristram Shandy* itself. The other is, of course, the cock-and-bull story, which Yorick praises in the very last sentence of the book.

5

English Transports and French Frictions

In 1762, a few years before Laurence Sterne began to think about the 'new work of four volumes' in July 1766 (L 284) which was to become the two-volume *Sentimental Journey* within the following one-and-a-half years, Jean-Jacques Rousseau published his four-volume *Émile ou de l'éducation*. Sterne, in Paris that year, failed to meet its author but bought and read the work in its first edition (LY 136, 163). In the fifth book of this treatise-cum-novel of education, he would have found an essay on the uses and abuses of travelling and travel writing. Here Rousseau categorizes various types of travelling and dismisses some of them: 'To travel for travelling's sake is to wander aimlessly, to be a vagabond [...]. I would instil into any young man embarking upon a journey a lively interest in educating himself.' He also compares and contrasts the travelling habits of the various European nations, in particular the French and the English: 'The English gentry and nobility travel, the French not at all; the French populace travels, the English not. [...] The English have the prejudice of arrogance, the French that of vanity.' Enumerating such cultural stereotypes and stereotypical differences, he hastens to add, however, that with the increasing numbers of travellers and the improved travel facilities in recent times the original characters of different peoples vanish from day to day and become for that reason ever more difficult to grasp. As races blend and peoples intermingle, those national differences which formerly struck the observer at first sight gradually disappear.[1]

Sterne's *Sentimental Journey* shares many of the concerns of

Rousseau's essay and stages them in the form of a fictional travelogue. For Yorick, 'The Sentimental Traveller' (*SJ* 11), as for Rousseau, the European countries are rapidly becoming less foreign and their peoples less strange or alien to each other. As he writes in his preface, commenting upon the present vogue of Continental and Grand Touring: 'It is an age so full of light, that there is scarce a country or corner of Europe whose beams are not crossed and interchanged with each other' (*SJ* 12). It is against this background of a growing – and often anxious – awareness of vanishing cultural difference between the European nations that Sterne constructs his discourse of national difference in *A Sentimental Journey*. As much as he insists upon human fellowship across borders, upon the shared humanity of all humankind and on the 'great – great SENSORIUM of the world' which envelops us all (*SJ* 117), he equally insistently dramatizes cultural difference and the frictions between rivalling national identities. From the first sentence –'They order, said I, this matter better in France' (*SJ* 3) – to the last episode, which entangles the travelling English gentleman with a Piedmontese lady and her Lyonoise maid in an imbroglio rich with cross-cultural erotic potential, Sterne has Yorick constantly play off against each other English and French temperaments, attitudes, customs, institutions and ways of life. And he does this not in the grand gestures of sweeping generalization to which the contemporary writers of Grand Tour travelogues were all too prone, but by observing and dramatizing cultural difference in tiny, yet telling, in luminous yet ludicrous details:

> I think I can see the precise and distinguishing marks of national character more in these nonsensical *minutiae*, than in the most important matters of state; where great men of all nations talk and stalk so much alike, that I would not give ninepence to chuse amongst them. (*SJ* 50)

It is in such minute details that he salvages a sense of difference between the European nations against the fears of an encroaching sameness spreading across a melting pot of Europe. Thus he contributes – in his own, more subtle, way than that of the ordinary Grand Tour writer – to a discourse of difference that highlights the peculiarities and distinguishing characteristics of the various nations – enhancing particularly those of his own nation – and keeps furnishing the nation states with a sense of cultural identity and political legitimacy.

Barely arrived in Paris, Yorick goes to a barber's to have his English wig attended to after the wear and tear of the journey (*SJ* 49–50) – an undertaking that is not without its humorously narrated cross-cultural frictions. 'Of course' his wig will not do for the more fashionable Paris, and the periwig-maker suggests a new French model – a model so elaborate and ornate that practically-minded Yorick fears that 'this buckle won't stand'. The barber's assurance that it will stand even if 'immerged [...] into the ocean' then triggers off further reflections upon cultural differences between the English and the French: where a London barber's point of reference would have been a mere 'pail of water' in the next room, wherein one could actually and empirically test the wig's standing power, his Parisian colleague resorts to rhetorical hyperbole, to 'the French sublime' of oceanic immersion, beyond experimental proof in a city a hundred miles from the sea. The English and the French are contrasted here in terms of simplicity vs. refinement and elaboration, practical-mindedness vs. fashionableness, empirical proof and understatement vs. rhetorical ostentation – all of them oppositions that have functioned as well-established auto- and heterostereotypes, or self-images and images of the other, in the cross-cultural exchanges between England and France ever since the Renaissance and which have contributed towards defining and stabilizing an English national identity by way of setting it off from the French and Continental other (and vice versa). Even the sexual or gendered subtext of this episode, which begins with the question whether the French buckle will 'stand' or not when immersed and is again strongly suggested in the italicized phrase summing up the episode – *'The French expression professes more than it performs'* – is part of this traditional discourse of difference and otherness: the English, as true men, *perform* where the French gentlemen in their effeminate refinement and politeness only *profess*; the French 'grandeur is *more* in the *word'*, the English more 'in the *thing'* (a notorious phallic innuendo). As much as Yorick parades his sublimated sentiments and sensibilities, he does not refrain from insisting upon his British masculinity and sexual potency every now and then.

Yorick's account of his journey through France strings together a whole series of such episodes dramatizing national difference and providing him with ever new occasions for fashioning his own cultural identity, for fashioning himself in his Englishness, against the background of what he constructs as 'typically French'. In this respect, he is in the same trade as his author (beyond the fact that they are both clergymen): Laurence Sterne also performed the 'typically English' eccentric to his Continental audiences with great aplomb and to great effect, and his works have survived both in England and abroad, amongst other things, also for being so quintessentially English.

France is used throughout as a mirror or sounding board, whose echoes reflect upon, and define by contrast, Yorick's Englishness: if the French philosophers – down to 'the most *physical precieuse'* lady of the Parisian salons – incline towards 'materialism' and tend to consider man – with La Mettrie (*L'homme machine*, 1747) – as a mechanical appliance or 'machine' (*SJ* 4), the English sentimental traveller celebrates what is beyond matter and mechanism, i.e. the human body as an organism alive and vibrant with sentiment and emotions, eloquent of the soul and transfused by divine sensibility. And the French may be 'the most polished people in the world' (*SJ* 83), more 'civilised and courteous' in their manners than the English, and they may even be 'renowned for sentiment and fine feelings' (*SJ* 3), yet their sentiments appear to be more a matter of fine words than true feelings, and their feelings more a matter of social agreeableness and refined etiquette than of spontaneous emotions, effusions and transports. The French as a nation are polished and polite – but 'to an excess', as Yorick argues in a conversation about national characteristics with the Count de B**** (*SJ* 89–91): to an excess that risks losing 'the *politesse de cœur*, which inclines men more to human actions, than courteous ones' and which is still preserved in England and among the English, who still retain 'that distinct variety and originality of character, which distinguishes them, not only from each other, but from all the world besides' (*SJ* 90). True sentimentalism, Yorick's sentimentalism, is thus constructed as an essential element of his Englishness, and he travels to France not to learn it but test it, and by testing to enlarge and refine it.

True sentimentalism can be at home only where freedom

reigns. And that is – according to Sterne and many other eighteenth-century English writers from Addison onwards – not in the absolutist monarchies on the Continent, but in England and Great Britain after the Glorious Revolution, where humane and reasonable laws and parliamentary control protect the citizens' rights, guarantee their liberty and allow for 'more wit and variety of character' (*SJ* 13). In France the royal *Droits d'aubaine* threaten the foreigner with loss of all his possessions (*SJ* 3), and lack of a passport may lead to his incarceration in the Bastille (*SJ* 67–91). To even dare to protest against the King of France's unlimited and arbitrary power turns '*ces Messieurs Anglois*' into '*gens très extraordinaires*', as the host exclaims in wonder at Yorick's, for an Englishman, very ordinary and commonsensical animadversions (*SJ* 69).

His encounter with the captive starling in his cage (*SJ* 71–5) stages this contrast between English liberties and French despotism in symbolic terms. The bird, like the traveller, is English and his repeated cries, 'I can't get out' (*SJ* 71), 'his little song for liberty, being in an *unknown* language at Paris' (*SJ* 74), find no echo in France – and that surely not only for linguistic reasons, as the more far-reaching reflections on slavery, which this encounter occasions (*SJ* 72–3), make sufficiently clear. They may be sentimental in the modern, pejorative sense of the word, yet the early abolitionist voice which Sterne raises here as elsewhere in his works[2] reveals the political implications and the potential political virulence of his sentimentalism. Though primarily a private cult of refined sensibility and pleasurably benevolent emotions, it can be readily extended into potentially political libertarian and egalitarian sympathies across ethnic, national, class and gender barriers. Sterne's easy relations with some of the *encyclopédistes* and other key intellectuals of the French Enlightenment in Paris and their enthusiastic reception of his works bear this out.

Sterne himself on his two Continental tours of 1762–4 and 1765–6 did not go to France and Italy as a Grand Tourist; he did not go there to see the sights and study the institutions, but with ulterior purposes – to regain his health and to increase his visibility and reap the harvest of his fame. Yet the two Continental travellers in his fictions, Tristram in *Tristram Shandy*, volume VII, and Yorick in *A Sentimental Journey*, are clearly cast in the role of the Grand Tourist or, rather, relate their experiences constantly to those scripted for them. The very title, *A Sentimental Journey through France and Italy*, alludes to the conventions of Grand Tour travel writing, in particular to Tobias Smollett's *Travels through France and Italy*, published in May 1766, a few months before Sterne first mentioned planning his 'new work'. He had actually met Smollett in the South of France (*LY* 168–9) and has him now appear in the new work under the transparent soubriquet 'Smelfungus' – together with another disgruntled Grand Tourist, 'Mundungus', perhaps Samuel Sharp, the author of *Letters from Italy*, also published in 1766 (*SJ* 28–9). Smelfungus, as well as Mundungus, follow the beaten track of the Grand Tour, 'looking neither to his right hand or his left, lest Love or Pity should seduce him out of his road' and, looking at all the sights with eyes 'discoloured and distorted' by 'the spleen and jaundice', he finds fault even with the Pantheon and the Venus of Medicis. No wonder all such a Grand Tourist can deliver in the end is 'the account of his miserable feelings' (*SJ* 29).

Yorick is a Grand Tourist of a different mettle and defines the difference of his sentimental mettle, like Tristram before him, in pointed deviations from the way Grand Tourists travelled and wrote their travels. Sterne engages here in a critical dialogue not only with Smollett and Sharp, but with one of the great European modes of travelling and genres of travel writing in the early modern period. It reaches back far beyond Sterne's immediate butts to, say, Thomas Nugent's *The Grand Tour* (1749), Joseph Addison's *Remarks on Several Parts of Italy* (1705), Gilbert Burnet's *Some Letters* (1686), Richard Lassels' *Voyage of Italy* (1670) and Thomas Coryate's *Crudities* (1611).[3] As a mode of travelling, the Grand Tour was a guided tour of about two years along a well-established route across the Continent, mainly France and Italy, on which, ever since the sixteenth century, young British gentlemen were taken as a kind of finishing school after university. The intention was to prepare them for public office and civic responsibilities by polishing their manners through contact with the cultures across the Channel, increasing their knowledge of foreign languages, topographies and institutions and complementing their classical and historical studies with first-hand impressions of the celebrated sites and sights. And the literature of the Grand Tour – the 'apodemic' texts discussing the uses of foreign travel and prescribing methodized frames for interacting with and observing the other, the guide books and travelogues canonizing routes and sights – underwrote the didactic and educational intentions of this English brand of *Bildungsreise*. Of course there were, from the beginning, dissenting voices that warned against the dangers of the young British gentleman learning nothing but the vices – Catholicism, atheism, licentiousness, effeminacy – from the more sophisticated neighbours and returning to England 'worse transformed than ever was any in *Circe*'s court' (Roger Ascham, *The Scholemaster*, 1570),[4] having 'gone native' and having lost their English mettle and masculinity or become mere 'coxcombs'[5] and apes of foreign fashions. The Grand Tourist, therefore, had to be carefully screened from too close a contact with the foreign and the foreigners and his gaze had to be blinkered, directed to a curriculum of canonized *videnda*.

All this is thoroughly subverted in Sterne's *Sentimental Journey*, the first fictionalized account of a Grand Tour. In repeated apodemic reflections and in his actual behaviour, Yorick proposes an alternative model and, indeed, his 'travels and observations' are 'altogether of a different cast from any of [his] fore-runners' (*SJ* 11). If his journey is a *Bildungsreise*, its educational intention is not the gathering of facts and information but an *éducation sentimentale*. As he explains to the Count de B****: ''tis a quiet journey of the heart in pursuit of NATURE, and those affections which arise out of her, which make us love each other – and the world, better than we do' (*SJ* 84–5). Nor does he waste his time studying and describing once again what has been studied and described already so often by other Grand Tourists. Unlike them, and like Tristram before him, he does not reduce the other country to a systematic catalogue of 'their laws – their religion – their government – their manufactures – their commerce – their finances' (*TS* VIII.xix.414) or an annotated enumeration of their curiosities, rarities and art treasures. He is not interested in their works of art but their hearts, particularly the female hearts:

> It is for this reason [...] that I have not seen the Palais royal – nor the Luxembourg – nor the Façade of the Louvre – nor have attempted to swell the catalogues we have of pictures, statues, and churches – I conceive every fair being as a temple, and would rather enter in, and

see the original drawings and loose sketches hung up in it, than the transfiguration of Raphael itself. (*SJ* 84)

And though he follows the route of the Grand Tour in its general direction towards the south, he allows himself to be sidetracked by any chance encounter, coincidence or whim. As he says himself: 'there is a fatality in it – I seldom go to the place I set out for' (*SJ* 78), and this constantly disrupts the linear teleology of the Grand Tour, right down to breaking off his account before he actually makes it into Italy, the ultimate destination and climax of the Tour. Thus he drifts, rather than travels across France – Rousseau's 'vagabond', indeed – and 'interests his heart in every thing, and [...], having eyes to see, what time and chance are perpetually holding out to him as he journeyeth on his way, misses nothing he can *fairly* lay his hands on' (*SJ* 28).

So, far from keeping the other at a safe distance, he constantly seeks contact, communication and communion with it. The series of sights that makes up the classical Grand Tour account is here transformed into a series of encounters, and these encounters with congenial souls extend across males and females of all classes and estates – from the Count de B**** to the countless 'grissets' and 'filles de chambre', from Madame de L*** and the Marquesina di F*** to poor Friar Lorenzo and the nameless Lyonois peasant so happy among his family. They all – to say nothing of Maria's little dog, the dead ass or the captive starling – engage his human interest, stimulate his affections and sympathies and put his sensibility to the test. It is this which makes him a sentimental traveller above all, and as such he is more concerned with his own sentiments than with the external reality the Grand Tourist observed and wrote his observations and remarks upon. Even at places where other travellers would only see a barren desert with nothing to observe, he 'would find out wherewith in it to call forth [his] affections' (*SJ* 28). His account, unlike that of the Grand Tourist, is self-consciously and programmatically subjective. On the other hand, it seeks to avoid the self-righteous and arrogant sense of superiority which limits and distorts other travellers' perceptions of the Continent and on which the discourse of difference in English Grand Tour writing is based. Of course, as we have seen, Yorick too is not without his own culturally prefabricated assumptions of what is 'typically French' and 'typically English' and where the English are superior to the French, and his prejudices also frame his perceptions and interactions; yet, at the same time, Sterne furnishes him with a – shall I say, 'hermeneutical'? – awareness of these processes of projection and with a greater openness towards the other, which allows him to see it in its positive as well as negative aspects and not only as a contrastive foil but also as an enriching complement to the self. Characteristically, this is put most succinctly by an anonymous French officer:

> Le POUR, et le CONTRE se trouvent en chaque nation; there is a balance, said he, of good and bad everywhere; and nothing but the knowing it is so can emancipate one half of the world from the prepossessions which it holds against the other – that the advantage of travel, as it regarded the sçavoir vivre, was by seeing a great deal both of men and manners; it taught us mutual toleration; and mutual toleration, concluded he, making a bow, taught us mutual love. (SJ 62–3)

There is another model of travelling and travel writing with which *A Sentimental Journey* is in dialogue: the picaresque narrative.[6] Sterne was not the only writer in the England of the eighteenth century to respond to this model in his own fiction: Defoe (*Moll Flanders*, 1722), Fielding (*Joseph Andrews*, 1742), Smollett (*Roderick Random*, 1748) and others preceded him in this. What their texts share with the Spanish picaresque novels from *Lazarillo de Tormes* (1553) to Cervantes's *Don Quixote* (1605, 1615) is the concept of fiction as a road show, a road movie, a loosely organized series of adventures along a road that does not follow a predetermined route, takes surprising or seemingly random turns and brings the traveller in contact with characters from all walks of life. Yorick, as a sentimental traveller, is, of course, devoid of the classical *picaro*'s cunning; he is innocent, rather, like Parzival or, to use a closer analogue, Voltaire's Candide. Nor is he a *picaro* or 'rogue' in the sociological sense of the word; he is not a destitute outsider to society but, as a clergyman of sufficient means, one of its pillars. Yet, travelling abroad, he takes a holiday from his secure place within society at home and that gives him the freedom to play the fool and vagabond, to perform as *picaro* to ever new audiences and let himself get entangled in ever new 'adventures' (SJ 28, 137).

Sterne's more immediate picaresque antecedent is, however, not the classical rogue tale of the *Lazarillo de Tormes* variety but Cervantes's *Don Quixote*. To him and his hero he had already repeatedly paid tribute in *Tristram Shandy*, most notably in the 'Invocation' to his 'gentle spirit of sweetest humour' (IX.xxiv.527), and in *A Sentimental Journey* Cervantes and Don Quixote are, after Shakespeare and his Yorick, the literary model most frequently referred or alluded to. Already in his apodemic preface on sentimental travelling Yorick quotes Sancho Panza's misgivings about all travel (*SJ* 12), and near the end, going once again out of his way to find Tristram's Maria, he identifies with 'the Knight of the Woeful Countenance, in quest of melancholy adventures' (*SJ* 113). The intertextual dialogue goes beyond such occasional references once Yorick travels together with his servant La Fleur: like Parson Adams and Joseph Andrews in Fielding's *History of the Adventures of Joseph Andrews and of his Friend Mr. Abraham Adams. Written in Imitation of the Manner of Cervantes, Author of 'Don Quixote'* before them, they travel in the wake of Don Quixote and Sancho Panza – full of highfalutin dreams and aspirations the one and, also erotically, more down-to-earth the other. If not a knight-errant like Don Quixote, he is Eros errant, and his ideals of divine sensibility are to him what the romances of knightly adventure and courtly love are to his Spanish model. This, of course, casts an ambiguous veil over his sentimental performances and, as with Don Quixote, we are never quite sure how to take them: as admirable aspirations or self-deluded folly; as seriously intended or as tongue-in-cheek histrionics or, even worse, Tartuffe-like hypocrisy; as endorsed by his author or ironically sent up by him. And critics have remained as divided about the wisdom of Sterne's sentimental traveller, who, after all, proudly bears the name of Shakespeare's fool, as they have about the *locura* or madness of Cervantes' Knight of the Woeful Countenance.[7]

More important than all these dialogues with the Grand Tourists, the picaresque tales of adventure, Cervantes and Shakespeare, is, however, Sterne's dialogue with himself here, the dialogue with both *The Journal to Eliza*, which he writes simultaneously with the *Journey*, and *Tristram Shandy*, the work-in-progress he interrupts to write his 'new work' as a new departure from it.

In many ways, the *Journey* is a sequel – or, alternatively, a 'prequel' – to *Tristram Shandy*: Yorick, the parson on the Shandy estate, reappears in it, promoted to the rank of protagonist, and as Yorick had died already in the first volume of *Tristram Shandy* (I.x) he seems to be strangely resurrected here. Yet Yorick's death in *Tristram Shandy* is only *narrated* early in the book; within the chronology of the story it is actually one of the latest events – occurring in 1748, it is postdated only by Tristram's 1760s tour of France in volume VII and, of course, by Tristram writing his 'Life and Opinions'. So, paradoxically, Yorick dies long before Tristram's tour and yet travels in his traces. Things are confusing, indeed, and Sterne wants them to be so.

The links between the two fictions go far beyond Yorick featuring in both of them. They are so numerous that the two can, to a certain extent, be considered as one work: everywhere *A Sentimental Journey* takes a knowledge of the Shandy household for granted and at places – most memorably in Yorick's encounter with Maria, which continues her melancholy story from *Tristram Shandy* (IX.xxiv.528–30) published the year before – it quite pointedly refers back to particular episodes in the previous nine volumes. More importantly still, it extends the 'laughing good temperd Satyre against Traveling' and Grand Tourists (*L* 231) in volume VII of *Tristram Shandy* to its own two volumes and replays many of the previous work's stylistic tricks and defamiliarizing narrative devices.

And yet, there is a markedly different tone and narrative texture to both works: *A Sentimental Journey* is less eccentric and more linear in its way of telling its story than *Tristram Shandy*, and the story it tells is less spiced with obscenity and salaciousness and richer in situations stirring tender emotions. To try, with the Victorian critics of the nineteenth and twentieth centuries, to explain this change in biographical terms, as the consequence of 'Sterne in Love' (with Eliza) and at death's door, does not get one very far; after all, Sterne had always been in love and was already under the shadow of imminent death when writing *Tristram Shandy*. His correspondence during the last one and a half years of his life tells a different story – the story of a supreme performer responding creatively to the responses of his audience.[8]

His contemporary readers and critics found the idiosyncratic narrative and meta-narrative games he played with them in *Tristram Shandy* increasingly repetitive and stale and the smuttiness increasingly off-putting; on the other hand, they thought his real talent for the pathetic, as it showed for them particularly impressively in the Le Fever episode (VI.vi–xiii), was wasted in a flood of scurrility. A long unsigned review (by Ralph Griffiths) of volumes VII and VIII in the *Monthly Review* of February 1765, cast in the form of a dialogue with the author, is indicative of this trend, which was to gather further strength with the publication of volume IX in January 1767:

> The Public, if I guess right, will have *had enough*, by the time they get to the end of your eighth volume. [...] Give up your Long Noses, your Quedlinbergs, and your Andoüillets. [...] One of our gentlemen once remarked, *in print*, Mr. Shandy – that he thought your excellence lay in the PATHETIC. I think so too. In my opinion, the little story of Le Fever has done you more honour than every thing else you have wrote, except the Sermons. Suppose you were to strike out a new plan? Give us none but amiable or worthy, or exemplary characters; or, if you will, to enliven the drama, throw in the *innocently humorous* [...] – awake our affections, engage our hearts – arouze, transport, refine, improve us. (CH 167–8)

The 'plan for something new, quite out of the beaten track' which Sterne has laid by February 1767 (L 301) appears to be a direct response to such appeals, and once he is seriously engaged in writing *A Sentimental Journey* – 'an Original work, and likely to take in all Kinds of readers' (L 393) – his correspondence becomes more explicit about how it differs from *Tristram Shandy*:

> I told you my design in it was to teach us to love the world and our fellow creatures better than we do [cf. *SJ* 85] – so it runs more upon those gentler passions and affections, which aid so much to it. (L 401)

He announces himself programmatically as the 'sentimental being' he has 'long been' and dissociates himself from the image people formed of him on the basis of *Tristram Shandy*: 'The world has imagined, because I wrote Tristram Shandy, that I was myself more Shandean than I really ever was' (L 402–3). And according to Richard Griffith, an acquaintance to whom he showed the new work-in-progress and who found that it 'has all the Humour and Address of the best Parts of Tristram, and is quite free from the Grossness of the worst', he even declared it 'his *Work of Redemption*' (LY 308). As such, it is 'a chaste book' –

and 'mercy on them that read it' and do not find it so, 'for they must have warm imaginations indeed!' (*L* 403) – and its two volumes are 'a *couple of as clean brats* as ever chaste brain conceiv'd', even if 'they are frolicksome too, *mais cela n'empeche pas*' (*L* 405).

Of course, as the overstated and playful tone of his declarations gives it already away: Reverend Sterne doth protest too much. *A Sentimental Journey* is not all chaste sentimentalism, and its frolicsomeness is not all innocent and clean. There still is, after all, '*Monsieur l'Abbé*' at the Opera comique, who has to hold up his hands so that the 'grissets' are safe from being touched up by him, or 'Madame de Rambouliet', who 'plucks her roses' in public (*SJ* 62–3). And, from Yorick finding himself intimately close together with Madame de L*** in the *désobligeant* coach at Calais, feeling the pulse and trying on a pair of gloves with the help of the beautiful *grissette* in Paris and tumbling upon his bed and upon the *fille de chambre*, to the very last moment of the book where he reaches out for another 'fille de chambre's – ', there are again and again situations as pregnant with, and suggestive of, sexual parts and sexual play as any in *Tristram Shandy*.

What we have here, then, rather than the clean change of heart so dear to the heart of the Victorian critic, is Sterne the versatile and ambidextrous performer experimenting towards a new balance of the erotic and the sentimental, of sentimentalism and ludicrous posturing, of pathos and bathos, of blood, laughs and tears – always ready, in case it should not work, 'to give up the Business of sentimental writing – & write to the Body' again, as he told an elusive correspondent of the last months of his life, his 'good dear girl, Hannah' (*L* 401). The sentimentality of his *Sentimental Journey* is, indeed, a performance[9] – as sentimentalism is in general. Emotions and affections may be unselfconscious, sentiment never is. The cult of sentiment and sensibility always involves an element of conscious self-staging, even if there is no further audience for it than the sentimentalist himself or herself relishing, and glorying in, an 'exquisite sensation' (*SJ* 43) or, alternatively, as is so often the case with Sterne and Yorick, stepping back from it and laughing at its very exquisiteness.

'Pray, Sir', Lady Bradshaigh famously asked Samuel Richardson in 1749, 'what, in your opinion, is the meaning of the word *sentimental*?' There is, she notes, a fashion of using it for 'everything clever and agreeable'.[10] And Sterne, more than one and a half decades later, still notes that 'notwithstanding they [the French] make such a pother about the *word*, they have no precise idea annex'd to it' (L 256). What the lady obviously had in mind was the word 'sentimental' as the adjective of the noun 'sentiment' in the now rather rare sense of a moral reflection, the succinct expression of an opinion or view as to what is right or agreeable (cf. *OED*, 'sentiment', 6), the expression of an emotion rather than the emotion itself.

Sterne's remark in his letter is actually occasioned by just such a sentiment, the French saying, '*l'amour n'est rien sans sentiment*'. This is a sentiment about sentiment, and Sterne seems to have been rather fond of it, as he re-used it in *A Sentimental Journey*. Here it becomes one of a string of sentiments that make up the French love letter copied by Yorick from a model provided for him by his servant La Fleur and sent to Madame de L***: 'L'amour n'est *rien* sans sentiment. Et le sentiment est encore *moins* sans amour' (*SJ* 47). Indeed, as this recycling of La Fleur's Corporal's love letter makes abundantly clear, love – at least in France – is nothing without the appropriate verbal profession of love. This is also the sense in which Yorick employed the word before in his flirtatious dialogue with Madame de L*** in the remise at Calais (*SJ* 26–7), when he takes exception to the French absurdity of wooing by gallant professions: 'To think of making love by *sentiment*!' He protests too much, however. As his very protest against sentiments is couched in the form of a series of sentiments, he does precisely what he rejects and 'makes love by sentiment' himself. It takes a woman, and a French-speaking lady at that, to point this out to him: 'Then I solemnly declare, said the lady, blushing – you have been making love to me all this while' (*SJ* 27).

In all these cases there is a semantic friction at work between the old, rhetorical sense of the word, the fine sentiments, and the more recently highlighted sense of actually felt tender sentiments or emotions of love, benevolence, generosity and pity. Love may be nothing without fine professions, but it is equally nothing without the authentic and active feelings that it is made up of. A gap opens up here between verbal profession and authentic emotion, between the expression of sentiments and their realization in deed, between the social performance and the interiority of the subject. And this gap lends itself readily to comic exploitation: Sheridan wrote a whole comedy about it, *The School for Scandal* (1777), and in Sterne's *Sentimental Journey* as well the semantic friction sparks off comic effects. There is, however, a crucial difference to the comedy of sentiments between the two: where, with Sheridan's characters, the social mask of fine sentiments can always be clearly distinguished from the authenticity of the emotion, with Sterne and his Yorick such a distinction collapses all too easily and all too frequently. Both his spoken or written sentiments and the sentimental vibrations of his body, the sensitive glances, the tender blushes and benevolent and sympathetic tears, are sincerely felt and a staged performance at one and the same time.

Let us take an example: Yorick, more than half in love with Madame de L***, fantasizes about the sad story of her woes which she has promised to tell him and for which he is prepared to go out of his way to her hometown Brussels:

> with what a moral delight will it crown my journey, in sharing in the sickening incidents of a tale of misery told to me by such a sufferer? to see her weep! And though I cannot dry up the fountain of her tears, what an exquisite sensation is there still left, in wiping them away from off the cheecks of the first and fairest of women, as I'm sitting with my handkerchief in my hand in silence the whole night besides her. (*SJ* 43)

Here, in what Yorick envisages as the culminating point of his sentimental journey and travelogue, all the ingredients of sentimentalism flow together and release an all-night flood of tears. The situation his fantasies focus upon is characteristically speechless: sentimentalism comes into its own after and beyond verbal communication, as an exchange of glances, touches and tears. The tears are, as always, a weak and innocent victim's tears – here, as so often and most memorably in the sentimental cameo piece of mad and lovelorn Maria (*SJ* 113–16) – a woman's tears, a suffering woman's tears, a fair and suffering woman's tears. Sentimentalism feeds on a weak victim's suffering it cannot relieve and delights in its own benevolent sympathy to the very extent that the suffering is undeserved and unrelievable.

The suffering female, together with the intimately secluded situation, give to Yorick's 'exquisite sensation' an emotional charge in which the sentimental and the erotic, sympathy and desire, intermingle inextricably. The lady weeps over her own sad story, and it is important for the intensity of the emotions released here that neither Yorick nor the reader know anything about her 'tale of misery'. Unheard melodies are sweeter, and so are unheard tales of misery, as they stimulate our imagination beyond any 'sickening incidents' and thus make the story and its emotions our own. Sentimentalism relies on fantasy and imagination, and it is therefore also important here that the story as well as the pathetic telling of the story and Yorick's 'exquisite sensation' at it are all of his own fantasy's making, a dream of displaced wishfulfilment in which her tears and his sympathetic glances freely commingle. Sentimental writing is, like the bawdy or pornographic 'writing to the body', a matter of stimulating suggestions that engage the (male) reader's imaginative cooperation in completing what is represented only in carefully selected parts. In this sense, *A Sentimental Journey* is uncomfortably close to the pornographic classic of Sterne's age, John Cleland's *Memoirs of a Woman of Pleasure* aka, *Fanny Hill* (1748–9). Cleland actually had found 'Sterne's bawdy' in the early volumes of *Tristram Shandy* 'too plain' (*LY* 92); he may have revised his opinion when it came to the later volumes and particularly to *A Sentimental Journey*, where sentiment and sexuality co-inhabit Sterne's text in a sophisticated fusion.

Cleland's text, of course, owns up to, or even acknowledges cheerfully, what Sterne's text denies that it intends, yet achieves precisely by denying it: the stimulation of the reader's sexual fantasies. Yorick's performance as a narrator is thus much more demanding than Cleland's: he must be knowing and appear innocent at the same time; he must believe in the sentimental sublimation of sexuality and yet show a deflating awareness of its make-believe. His promises of the 'moral delight', which the writing and the reading of his stories will convey, must be persuasive enough, and the titillation of his and his reader's imagination with delights of another kind dexterous enough, to turn his 'hypocrite lecteur' into his 'semblable', his 'frère' (Baudelaire, *Les fleurs du mal*, 'Au Lecteur'). These conflicting demands and claims are frequently laid bare in moments of self-censorship, of ironic self-distancing, of bathos, or humorous deflation. Our passage culminates in just such a moment of self-awareness, which disrupts his sentimental fantasy:

> There was nothing wrong in the sentiment [the emotion? the verbal expression given to the emotion? both?]; and yet I instantly reproached my heart with it in the bitterest and most reprobate of expressions. (*SJ* 43)

It is, as so often, the thought of his Dulcinea, Eliza, that cuts across Yorick's titillating fantasy as well as his complacent visions of moral delight here, but surely the author's self-monitoring irony has preceded, and exceeds, his character's self-censuring here as elsewhere. The extremes to which he allows his protagonist to carry his extravagant fantasies put them at an ironic distance and turn Yorick's sentimental performance into a parody of itself, and even 'the bitterest and most reprobate of expressions' which follow promptly upon the sentimental debauch are, in their superlative hyperbole, shown up for what they also are – more, and mere, 'sentiments'.

Yorick is transported across France from one such 'transport' to the next, from the encounter with Friar Lorenzo in the streets of Calais to the shared night in one bedroom with the Piedmontese lady near Lyons. And in all these 'transports of this kind', in which 'the heart, in spite of the understanding, will always say too much' (*SJ* 44), his sentiments during the encounter as well as his sentiments while writing and narrating them – and, of course, also his reader's sentiments – are put to the test of comic friction. What Sterne puts to the test in the carefully arranged oscillations between sentiment and humour, tears and laughter, is, however, not only Yorick's sentimental-ism, the moving spectacles of benign generosity and tender sympathy he stages: it is a whole cult and culture of sensibility and a pervasive discourse of sentiment. They are not of Sterne's creating but go back at least to the beginning of the century, though undoubtedly Sterne was crucial in fashioning them persuasively for his contemporaries and the following one or two generations both in England and abroad.

This cult and this culture synthesize diverse ingredients, latitudinarian theology with its reappraisal of the affective dimensions in religious worship and charitable practice being one of them[11] and the growing unease about rationalist reductions of reality to mere matter and mechanism another. More important, however, was a new kind of moral philosophy which first surfaced in the writings of a deist aristocrat, Anthony Ashley Cooper, Third Earl of Shaftesbury.[12] In his *Characteristics of Men, Manners, Opinions, Times* (1711) and other writings, Shaftesbury tried to work out a secularized system of ethics based on the innate goodness and moral sense of man, whose natural affections (love, human sympathy, pity, delight in others' welfare; kindness, affability, candour, generosity...) and whose active benevolence find their gratification in the pleasurable awareness of his own virtue and the sense of chiming in with divine Nature.

At first sight, this appears to be impeccably egalitarian and philanthropic, yet a closer look reveals the class-based nature of Shaftesbury's 'philosophical rhapsodies' over general bene-volence and generous feelings. They are framed throughout by equally vociferous defences of aristocratic privilege which make it sufficiently clear that goodness is innate and natural only to persons of birth and rank. Shaftesbury's philosophy of a moral sense residing in natural affections actually identifies worth with birth and conflates morals with aristocratic manners. His 'sentiment of MORALS'[13] is a constituent part of refined aristo-cratic manners, a mark of distinction that legitimizes its privileges, power and liberties. On the other hand, his rhetoric of natural affections and innate virtues recommended Shaftes-bury's philosophy to bourgeois writers such as Addison or Steele, to whom, paradoxically, it opened up the possibility of promoting the virtues and merits of the middle class. By universalizing Shaftesbury's natural affections they sought to enlarge the ranks of 'the better sort', striving to include the minor gentry as well as the professions by virtue of demon-strated good-nature and sensibility. Their middle-class 'men of feeling', by displaying refined sensibility and generous bene-volence, staged themselves as aristocrats *honoris causae*, as aristocrats of feeling. The 'theatrics of sentimentalism'[14] and the culture of sensibility should, therefore, be regarded as one of the ways in which the bourgeoisie challenged aristocratic prerogatives and asserted its own leading role in society as a better and more meritorious kind of aristocracy. This was not a matter of imitation but of emulation, the attempt to outrefine and moralize the aristocratic codes of virtue and manners; it was not a matter of merely appropriating Shaftesbury's discourses of sentiments and affections but of redefining them in an attempted reconciliation with traditional Christian notions and values.

This 'baptized' discourse of sensibility, as inherited by Sterne and further refined and tested in the alembic of his fictions, has a high moral and religious tone to it. Nowhere does it rise to higher transports than in Yorick's celebrated invocation to 'Dear sensibility'. It comes immediately after his particularly moving encounter with the thrice abandoned Maria – abandoned by the beloved, by her goat, and by reason – which has stirred his tender feelings of sympathy and longing to unprecedented heights:

> Dear sensibility! Source inexhausted of all that's precious in our joys, or costly in our sorrows! thou chainest thy martyr down upon his bed of straw – and 'tis thou who lifts him up to HEAVEN – eternal fountain of our feelings! – 'tis here I trace thee – and this is thy divinity which stirs within me —— not, that in some sad and sickening moments, *'my soul shrinks back upon herself, and startles at destruction'* – mere pomp of words! – but that I feel some generous joys and generous cares beyond myself – all comes from thee, great – great SENSORIUM of the world! which vibrates, if a hair of our heads but falls upon the ground, in the remotest desert of thy creation. (*SJ* 117)

The ecstatic rhetoric is sheer Shaftesbury, reminding one, for instance, of the exalted and breathless apostrophes to 'glorious nature! supremely fair, and sovereignly good! all-loving and all-lovely, all-divine!' in the Earl's *Moralists: A Philosophical Rhapsody*.[15] The religious, the sentimental, and the erotic are inextricably entwined in Yorick's emotional and rhetorical transport here and together they support a moral vision that extends from the individual and the social to the cosmic sphere: (1) Sentiment and sensibility alone can bridge the gap between soul and body and make the *individual* a complete person that thinks and feels and is aware of his or her own feelings. They reside as a potential in each person and need to be activated in acts of kindness, benevolence, and uncalculating generosity and feelings of tender sympathy and love, the beauty of which is its own reward. (2) In this they open up the individual to the other and knit *society* together by transforming it into a community of all feeling and mutually sympathizing beings. Under these auspices of an innate, internalized, and spontaneous moral sense it is no longer necessary to enforce laws upon the individual from the outside. This implies a utopian or millenarian perspective in which the whole state apparatus of disciplining and coercion becomes superfluous and may vanish together with all hierarchies of class, power and possessions. (3) Such a society would then be modelled on the order and harmony of the cosmos as one 'great – great SENSORIUM', which vibrates with the goodness of God and whose vibrations find their echo in the vibrating sensibilities of all his beings from the highest to the lowest. Sterne's metaphor of the sensorium, in which and through which our emotions vibrate, may derive from Addison, who reminds us of Newton calling the infinite space of the cosmos 'the *Sensorium* of the Godhead'.[16]

In spite of all the egalitarian pathos of this and similar passages in *A Sentimental Journey*, Yorick takes social distinctions and privileges for granted. Even where he demonstratively celebrates the virtues of the lower orders – as, for instance, in the very next episode, in which a French peasant's family is held up as a shining example of benevolent love and mutual sympathy and in which their prayer and dance enact his vision of harmony (*SJ* 118–20) – he dramatizes the difference between 'an illiterate peasant' and the self-conscious sensibilities of the educated middle-class sentimental traveller. The indigence and suffering of the poor provide him, as the sentimentalist in general, with occasions for sentimental performances but do not disturb his fundamental sense that inequality is part of the natural and divinely ordained scheme of things. He is generously free with his sympathy, though more careful with the charity he doles out to beggars or chambermaids, but restricts the further-reaching egalitarian implications of a universal brotherhood of sentient beings to private fantasies. As with Henry Mackenzie's 'Man of Feeling' (*The Man of Feeling*, 1771), his generosity is riddled with the paradox inherent in the economy of all private charity: you have to be thrifty and sparing with your charity to be able to continue to be charitable; he is, however, more successful than Mackenzie's protagonist in suppressing an awareness of these contradictions.

As with the social injustices of class distinctions, so with the unequal dispensations of the gender order: as much as sentimentalist writers can claim to have contributed towards smoothing out the aggressively masculinist ethos of an older aristocracy and reappraising the particularly feminine virtues and values of tender affections, and as much as the cult of sentimentalism has furnished bourgeois and gentry society with feminized models of behaviour, they continued to take the hierarchy of male over female for granted. Even where Yorick, bursting into a flood of tears over Friar Lorenzo's grave, admits, or rather, proudly proclaims himself to be 'as weak as a woman' (*SJ* 21), this defines women as weak by nature, and his interactions with women and his transports over them underwrite their traditional roles as objects of male desire in need of male protection. It is he who eroticizes their suffering, vulnerability or – particularly with respect to women below him in class – their dependence on, and exposedness to, male mastery. They are to him 'the sex' indeed, as he repeatedly calls them (e.g. *SJ* 21, 36, 95) in accordance with a semantic gender code that reduces women to their sexuality, and it is from them that the sexual allure always emanates, whether he imagines them as pastorally innocent or always all too compliant. As sentimental lover he is always the seduced, not the seducer, and he proves the precarious masculinity of a sentimental and valetudinarian Englishman of middle age by feeling 'The Temptation' (*SJ* 91–3) and resisting to it ('The Conquest', *SJ* 94). The Man of Feeling may be self-consciously effeminate – but only to prove that he is the better woman.

Far from actually challenging class and gender hierarchies and social and political injustice, the sentimentalist's good-natured benevolence and tender sympathies remain contained within a private, 'miniaturized' world of intimate interactions, physiological micro-sensations located in the nerves, fibres and blood vessels, and of rarified and self-delighted imaginings.[17] Far from doing away with aristocratic elitism, he creates a new kind of elite and arrogates its prerogatives – the aristocracy of the few, the tender few, who feel, know that they feel, delight in their own feelings and know how to 'translate' (*SJ* 56–8, 110) others' body language of feeling into an emotionally vibrant text; an aristocracy which the readers – 'the few who feel to analyse' (*SJ* 20) – are invited to join. And they join precisely to the extent that they manage to conflate their experience of reading with the experiences represented. As Sterne wrote to one of them, Dr John Eustace, a few weeks before his death:

> a true feeler always brings half the entertainment along with him. His own ideas are only call'd forth by what he reads, and the vibrations within, so entirely correspond with those excited, 'tis like reading *himself* and not the *book*. (*L* 411)

In all this, and in spite of all this, an element of *mauvaise foi* keeps lingering over Yorick's sentimental performances, an element which Virginia Woolf, if perhaps not the first to note, was the first to pin down precisely.[18] What she tended to overlook, however, are the many intriguingly intricate ways in which Sterne dramatizes the *mauvaise foi* by framing Yorick's sensations and sentiments ironically, by comic deflation and bathos, by innuendoes that suggest readings at variance with the self-understanding of this connoisseur of sentiments and *nouveaux frissons*, by a fragmentation of the narrative that leaves room for the reader's imagination or leaves him in midair. To give a tiny example: the Maria episode culminates in a particularly exalted transport of sympathetic sentiments, in which Yorick fantasizes about providing a home for the 'poor luckless maiden': 'she should *not only eat of my bread and drink of my cup*'. Even Yorick's invocation of the Bible [2 Samuel 9:7] here cannot delete the erotic connotations of his dream. It is, after all, a dream of cohabitation with a woman whom he regards as 'of the first order of fine forms – affliction had touch'd her looks with something that was scarce earthly – still she was feminine'. After such an introduction the very last word of his fantasy comes with a deeply ironic friction to it, as the last, vain, attempt to defuse the erotic tension: 'Maria should lay in my bosom, and be unto me as a daughter' (*SJ* 116). And, of course, he does nothing to relieve her suffering, and leaves nothing to her beyond the fine sentiments about 'Dear sensibility!', which quickly turn from the moving figure 'sitting pensive under her poplar' to fantasies about 'the roughest peasant', whose gentle heart bleeds to death with the piteous spectacle of 'the lacerated lamb of another's flock' bleeding to death (*SJ* 117).

Yorick's sentimental performances, his moments of self-irony and Sterne's deflating narrative frames round them both conceal and reveal the ideological underpinnings of the bourgeois ideology of sympathy and benevolence. It is this constant oscillation between blindness and insight which has kept *A Sentimental Journey* alive and a pleasure across the centuries, even if Sterne has no alternative to offer to the sentimentalism it puts to the test and finds insufficient. Yorick's sentimentality remains palatable, even delightful, to us to the extent to which his and his author's comic detachment manage to anticipate our own misgivings, to the extent to which we can recognize our own sense of disintegrated subjectivity in the plurality of roles the traveller, the narrator and the author perform, and to the extent to which we can sympathize with Sterne's irony as the only form of sincerity left to him.

Many of the early readers and users of *A Sentimental Journey* saw things differently. They could do without what is our delight: the irony, the bathos, the comedy of sentiment. For them the sentiment sufficed and they endorsed it whole-heartedly, singling out for special praise the cameo pieces – Yorick and Friar Lorenzo exchanging their snuffboxes (*SJ* 19–21), the German traveller grieving over his dead ass (*SJ* 39–41), the captive starling (*SJ* 72–5), and, of course, mad Maria and her faithful dog Sylvio under the poplar tree (*SJ* 113–16). Such purple passages were frequently anthologized or imitated in popular miscellanies or morally edifying magazines, and even parodies fed parasitically upon their sentiments and contrib-uted towards Sterne's reputation as the most refined of all sentimentalists.[19] Some of these episodes provided artists with moving *sujets* for drawings, etchings or paintings, as, for instance, Joseph Wright of Derby's beautiful genre piece *Maria From Sterne* (1781; Derby Museum and Art Gallery), which decorates the cover of 'our' World's Classics edition (cf. p. viii) of the *Journey*. And, going beyond such textual and pictorial uses, at least one of the pathetic episodes was actually translated into a social ritual: in Germany, where Bode's translation of *A Sentimental Journey* contributed the new and beautiful word 'empfindsam' to my language, it launched a veritable cult of 'Empfindsamkeit' among certain artists and their gentry audiences, Lorenzo's snuffbox became a shibboleth of tender sensibility. The anacreontic poet Johann Georg Jacobi sent one inscribed with 'Pater Lorenzo' to his friend and fellow poet Johann Wilhelm Ludwig Gleim in spring 1769; an accompanying letter, which was also published in the Hamburg-Correspondent, set up Yorick's generous offer of his tortoise snuffbox for Father Lorenzo's horn one as a model of sentimental exchanges of gifts. Some clever merchants promptly commodified the gesture and produced 'Lorenzo snuffboxes' to sell them successfully all over German-speaking Europe and as far as Livonia. Moritz and Christina von Brühl even had a 'Lorenzo-Hut' and a tombstone to Sterne's Franciscan friar erected in the park on their Seifersdorf estate near Dresden, where they performed the rites of sentimental friendship with their coterie of artists and gentry neighbours![20]

In such recyclings and performances 'Sterne's fragmentary text became famous for a certain kind of fragment'.[21] The sentimental text is by its very nature fragmented and episodic – a series of momentary transports and frictions rather than a continuous plot.[22] What is introduced at the very beginning of this series, when Yorick first unfeelingly rejects the French and Catholic friar Lorenzo's plea for charity, as a kind of 'Bildungsroman' avant la lettre –

> I have behaved very ill; said I within myself; but I have only just set out upon my travels; and shall learn better manners as I get along. (SJ 8)

– actually never takes off on the teleological trajectory of a 'Bildungsroman'. There is nothing that Yorick would or could learn on 'his quiet journey of the heart in pursuit of NATURE' (SJ 84), nor does he become better and more mature or gain in self-knowledge on his quest. Each episode, each fragment in this series of encounters, each transport and each friction, each of these 'cases' of conscience or of delicacy (SJ 96, 120) can only demonstrate anew the man of feeling's good nature and stage anew the unresolvable contradictions of his benevolent performances. Such a narrative 'can reach no conclusion; it can only stop'.[23]

And it is with, and as, a fragment that it finally comes to a stop. The very last episode in Yorick's journey – a journey which began and will end as a fragment in the middle of a sentence, a gesture and the Grand Tour to Italy, a journey which has left so many situations incomplete and has foregrounded its own fragmentary nature by two embedded fragments (*SJ* 34–5, 101–7) – is again occasioned by a fragment: quite literally a 'fragment' of rock (*SJ* 121) obstructing his way between St Michael and Madane and leading him to a one-bedchamber inn and to the last, most delicate and most dramatically inconclusive sample of erotic friction.

Sterne's not very famous last words (*LY* 327) are the most trenchant comment I would know for this sense of a fragmentary ending, be it the ending of a text or a life: *'Now it is come'*.

Notes

CHAPTER 1: SWIFTLY STERNEWARD

1. For the German reception of Sterne cf. Bernhard Fabian, 'Tristram Shandy and Parson Yorick among some German Greats', in Arthur H. Cash and John M. Stedmond (eds.), *The Winged Skull: Papers from the Laurence Sterne Bicentenary Conference* (London: Methuen, 1971), 194–209. Cf. also the forthcoming volume: John Neubauer and Peter de Voogd (eds.), *The Reception of Laurence Sterne in Europe* (London: Athlone).

2. Cf. Alice Green Fredman, *Diderot and Sterne* (New York: Columbia University Press, 1955), and Rainer Warning, *Illusion und Wirklichkeit in 'Tristram Shandy' und 'Jacques le Fataliste'* (München: Fink, 1965).

3. I quote R. J. Hollingday's translation from Melvyn New, *'Tristram Shandy': A Book for Free Spirits* (New York: Twayne, 1994), 16. As New's subtitle already suggests, his study is very much in a Nietzschean vein, exploring 'Sterne's meaning for a modern world permeated in immeasurable ways by the Nietzschean presence' (p. 17).

4. William M. Thackeray, *The English Humourists and The Four Georges*, ed. Walter Jerrold (London: Dent, 1912), 239.

5. Georg Lukács, 'Reichtum, Chaos und Form – Ein Zwiegespräch über Laurence Sterne', in *Die Seele und die Formen: Essays* (Berlin: Fleischel, 1911), 265–323.

6. English translations: Viktor Shklovsky, 'Sterne's Tristram Shandy: A Stylistic Commentary', in Lee T. Lemon and Marion J. Reis (eds.), Russian Formalist Criticism: Four Essays (Lincoln, NE.: University of Nebraska Press, 1965), 25–57; the 1929 version from *0 Teorii Prozy* (The Theory of Prose) is readily available in John Traugott (ed.), *Laurence Sterne: A Collection of Critical Essays* (Englewood Cliffs, NJ: Prentice-Hall, 1968), 66–89. For Shklovsky on Sterne see Ruth Whittaker, *Tristram Shandy* (Milton Keynes: Open University Press, 1988), 72–5.

7. 'A Parodying Novel', 89.

8. For this and further Sterne references in *Finnegans Wake*, cf. James S. Atherton, *The Books at the Wake* (London: Faber, 1959), 123.

9. Virginia Woolf, 'The *Sentimental Journey*', in *The Common Reader, Second Series* (London: Hogarth Press, 1932), 78–85; repr. in Gerd Rohmann (ed.), *Laurence Sterne: Wege der Forschung* (Darmstadt: Wissenschaftliche Buchgesellschaft, 1980), 57–63, here 58–9.

10. Thomas Mann, 'The Theme of the Joseph Novels', in *Thomas Mann's Addresses: Delivered to the Library of Congress, 1942–1949* (Washington, DC: Library of Congress, 1963), 12–13.

11. Milan Kundera, 'Afterword: A Talk with the Author by Philip Roth', in M. Kundera, *The Book of Laughter and Forgetting* (Harmondsworth: Penguin, 1983), 231.

12. Milan Kundera, *Jacques and his Master* (London: Faber, 1986), 12–13.

13. Cf. Salman Rushdie, *East, West* (London: Jonathan Cape, 1994), 83, and Walter Göbel and Damian Grant, 'Salman Rushdie's Silver Medal', in David Pierce and Peter de Voogd (eds.), *Laurence Sterne in Modernism and Postmodernism* (Amsterdam: Rodopi, 1996), 87–98. Further articles on Sterne and Modernism, by Robert Gorham Davis, Denis Donogue and Helen Moglen, are in Cash and Stedmond (eds), *The Winged Skull*, 21–75.

14. Harold Bloom (ed.), *Laurence Sterne's 'Tristram Shandy'* (London: Chelsea House, 1987), 1.

15. William Hazlitt, in *Lectures on the English Comic Writers* (1819); Alan B. Howes (ed.), *Sterne: The Critical Heritage* (London: Routledge & Kegan Paul, 1971), 361.

16. For 'metafiction' as a useful frame for reading Sterne cf. Linda Hutcheon, *Narcissistic Narrative: The Metafictional Paradox* (London: Methuen, 1984).

17. For bibliographical references cf. my 'Select Bibliography' at the end of this book. The preponderance of American contributions to Sterne studies has already been noted, with a certain acrimony, in Margaret R. B. Shaw, *Laurence Sterne: The Making of a Humorist, 1713–1762* (London: The Richards Press, 1957), pp. ix–xi.

18. F. R. Leavis, *The Great Tradition* (London: Chatto & Windus, 1948), 2, note 2.

19. Herbert Read (ed.), *A Sentimental Journey* (London: Scholartis Press, 1929); repr. in H. Read., *The Sense of Glory: Essays in Criticism* (Cambridge: Cambridge University Press, 1929), 123–51.

20. John Preston, *The Created Self: The Reader's Role in Eighteenth-Century Fiction* (London: Heinemann, 1970); A. D. Nuttall, *A Common Sky: Philosophy and the Literary Imagination* (London: Chatto & Windus, 1974); Janet Todd, *Sensibility: An Introduction* (London: Methuen, 1986).

21. Henri Fluchère, *Laurence Sterne, de l'homme à l'œuvre* (Paris: Gallimard, 1961); extracts of it, translated by Barbara Bray, appeared as *Laurence Sterne: From Tristram to Yorick*. (Oxford: Oxford University Press, 1965).

22. John Traugott (ed.), *Laurence Sterne: A Collection of Critical Essays* (Englewood Cliffs, NJ: Prentice-Hall, 1968), 148–67; Melvyn New (ed.), *Laurence Sterne: 'Tristram Shandy': Contemporary Critical Essays* (London: Macmillan, 1992), 17–35; the article was first published in *Essays in Criticism*, 1 (1951), 225–48. For Northrop Frye, cf. his *Anatomy of Criticism: Four Essays* (Princeton, NJ: Princeton University Press, 1957), 308–25.

23. D. W. Jefferson, *Laurence Sterne* (London: Longman, 1954).

24. This view is shared by Jonathan Lamb, *Sterne's Fiction and the Double Principle* (Cambridge: Cambridge University Press, 1989), 1–2.

CHAPTER 2: LIFE AND OPINIONS

1. For Reynold's portrait, cf. the trenchant in-depth interpretation in Werner Busch, *Das sentimentalische Bild: Die Krise der Kunst im 18. Jahrhundert und die Geburt der Moderne* (München: Beck, 1993), 395–404.

2. John Croft, 'Anecdotes of Sterne vulgarly Tristram Shandy', in W. A. S. Hewins (ed.), *Whiteford Papers, Being the Correspondence and other Manuscripts of Colonel Charles Whiteford and Caleb Whiteford from 1739 to 1810* (Oxford: Oxford University Press, 1898), 223–35, here 231.

3. I am indebted for this to Max Byrd, *Tristram Shandy* (London: George Allen & Unwin, 1985), 1.

4. Melvyn New, Preface, in M. New (ed.), *The Sermons of Laurence Sterne: The Notes*, The Florida Edition, vol. 5 (Gainesville: University of Florida Press, 1996), p. xiv.

5. New, Preface, *The Sermons*, p. xv.

6. Melvyn New (ed.), 'Sterne's Rabelaisian Fragment: A Text from the Holograph Manuscript', *PMLA*, 87 (1972), 1083–92.

7. The text, parts of which had first been published by Eliza Draper in *Letters from Yorick to Eliza* (1773), was rediscovered in the late nineteenth century and was first made available in Wilbur L. Cross (ed.), *The Complete Works and Life of Laurence Sterne* (New York: Taylor, 1904).

8. The informant is Richard Griffith, who met Sterne in autumn 1767 (*L* 399).

9. Elizabeth Kraft, *Laurence Sterne Revisited* (New York: Twayne, 1996), 5.

10. For Beckett and Sterne, see Hugh Kenner, *Flaubert, Joyce and Beckett: The Stoic Comedians* (Boston: Beacon Press, 1962), and John Fletcher,

The Novels of Samuel Beckett (London: Chatto & Windus, 1964).

11. Leigh A. Ehlers's attempt – in 'Mrs. Shandy's "Lint and Basilicon": The Importance of Women in *Tristram Shandy*', *South Atlantic Review*, 46:1 (1981), 61–75 – at turning *Tristram Shandy* into a 'woman's book', in which their 'untapped, restorative powers' are marginalized by the Shandy males to their own cost, is a laudible, though not utterly convincing effort to reclaim Sterne for feminism.

12. The homoerotic dimension is insisted upon, with particular reference to Yorick and La Fleur, by Eve Kosofsky Sedgwick in 'Sexualism and the Citizen of the World: Wycherley, Sterne, and Male Homosocial Desire', *Critical Inquiry*, 11 (1984), 226–45.

13. James A. Work (ed.), 'Introduction', *The Life and Opinions of Tristram Shandy* (New York: Odyssey, 1940), p. lx.

14. The omnipresence of sexuality and the whole gamut of its forms is perceptively explored in Frank Brady, '*Tristram Shandy*: Sexuality, Morality, and Sensibility', *Eighteenth-Century Studies*, 4 (1970), 41–56; repr. in Melvyn New (ed.), '*Laurence Sterne: 'Tristram Shandy'*: Contemporary Critical Essays, New Casebooks (London: Macmillan, 1992), 77–93.

15. For a good summary of Sterne's theological position, see Elizabeth Kraft, *Laurence Sterne Revisited* (New York: Twayne, 1996), 24–48; the introduction and notes to M. New (ed.), *The Sermons*, vols. 4 and 5 (Gainesville: University of Florida Press, 1996) are also extremely helpful.

16. For Sterne's political position, see Lewis P. Curtis, *The Politics of Laurence Sterne* (Oxford: Oxford University Press, 1929).

17. Melvyn New (ed.), *The Sermons of Laurence Sterne: The Notes* (Gainesville: University of Florida Press, 1996), vol. 5, pp. 205–14).

18. I am thinking in particular of Arthur Hill Cash's trend-setting study *Sterne's Comedy of Moral Sentiment: The Ethical Dimension of the 'Journey'* (Pittsburgh, PA.: Duquesne University Press, 1966).

19. Cash, *Sterne's Comedy*, 53, 55, 105.

20. See Melvyn New, '*Tristram Shandy': A Book for Free Spirits* (New York: Twayne, 1994), 3. In the following I am also indebted to New's succinct introductory chapter, 'The Milieu of *Tristram Shandy*', 3–8.

21. See John M. Stedmond, *The Comic Art of Laurence Sterne: Convention and Innovation in 'Tristram Shandy' and 'A Sentimental Journey'* (Toronto: University of Toronto Press, 1976), 49–54.

22. This crucial difference is problematically played down in Melvyn New's influential attempt – in *Laurence Sterne as Satirist: A Reading of 'Tristram Shandy'* (Gainesville: University of Florida Press, 1969) – to locate Sterne 'in the mainstream of the conservative, moralistic Augustan tradition' (p. 1).

23. For D. W. Jefferson, who first drew attention to this tradition, see ch. 1, note 28.
24. Some of these relations between Romantic aesthetics and Sterne have been sketched on a European scale in Peter Conrad, *Shandyism: The Character of Romantic Irony* (Oxford: Basil Blackwell, 1978).

CHAPTER 3: WRITING THE HOBBY-HORSE

1. Wayne C. Booth, 'The Self-Conscious Narrator in Comic Fiction before *Tristram Shandy*, *PMLA* 67 (1952), 163-85; repr. in Melvyn New (ed.), *Laurence Sterne: 'Tristram Shandy': Contemporary Critical Essays* (London: Macmillan, 1992), 36-59.
2. See ch. 1, note 28.
3. John Traugott, *Tristram Shandy's World: Sterne's Philosophical Rhetoric* (Berkeley: University of California Press, 1954).
4. Northrop Frye, *Anatomy of Criticism: Four Essays* (Princeton, NJ: Princeton University Press, 1957).
5. See ch. 2, note 20.
6. Frye, *Anatomy of Criticism*, 312.
7. Henry Fielding, *Joseph Andrews*, ed. R. F. Brissenden (Harmondsworth: Penguin, 1977), 25.
8. For a study of Sterne's fictions in the context of eighteenth-century (auto-)biography, see Clarence Tracy, 'As Many Chapters as Steps', in Arthur H. Cash and John M. Stedmond (eds.), *The Winged Skull: Papers from the Laurence Sterne Bicentenary Conference* (London: Methuen, 1971), 97–111.
9. See also Peter Conrad, *Shandyism: The Character of Romantic Irony* (Oxford: Blackwell, 1978), 43.
10. Lodwick Hartley, *Laurence Sterne in the Twentieth Century: An Essay and a Bibliography of Sternean Studies: 1900–65* (Chapel Hill, NC: University of North Carolina Press, 1966), 69.
11. For an excellent *tour d'horizon* of current concepts of performance and performativity in anthropology, philosophy, linguistics, economics and postmodernist gender and theatre studies see Marvin Carlson, *Performance: A Critical Introduction* (London: Routledge, 1996), ch. 1.
12. Virginia Woolf, 'The *Sentimental Journey*' (see above ch. 1, note 9), 58; cf. also Roger B. Moss, 'Sterne's Punctuation', *Eighteenth-Century Studies*, 15 (1981), 179–200.
13. I borrow this example from Max Byrd, '*Tristram Shandy*' (London: George Allen & Unwin, 1985), 24–5, who borrowed it in turn from the *Illustrations of Sterne* (2nd edn 1812) by John Ferriar, that great

detector of Sternean borrowings.

14. For the discussion about Sterne's fictions as finished, incomplete or fragments, see Wayne C. Booth, 'Did Sterne Complete *Tristram Shandy?'*, *Modern Philology* 48 (1951), 172–83; Marcia Allentuck, 'In Defense of an Unfinished *Tristram Shandy*: Laurence Sterne and the *Non Finito'*, in Arthur H. Cash and John M. Stedmond (eds.), *The Winged Skull*, 145–55; Elizabeth W. Harries, 'Sterne's Novels: Gathering Up the Fragments', *English Literary History*, 49 (1982), 35–49, repr. in Melvyn New (ed.), *Laurence Sterne: 'Tristram Shandy'. Contemporary Critical Essays* (London: Macmillan, 1992), 94–110.

15. Thomas Mann, Preface to *Stories of Three Decades*, trans. H. T. Lowe-Porter (New York: Alfred A. Knopf, 1936), p. vi.

16. See Fritz Gysin, *Model as Motif in 'Tristram Shandy'* (Berne: A. Francke, 1983).

17. See Wolfgang Iser, *Laurence Sternes 'Tristram Shandy': Inszenierte Subjektivität* (Munich: Wilhelm Fink, 1987), ch. 2.2; English version, *Laurence Sterne: 'Tristram Shandy'*, trans. David Henry Wilson (Cambridge: Cambridge University Press, 1988).

18. Sterne may have come across an extended and witty use of the writing/riding trope in Shaftesbury's 'Miscellaneous Reflections'; cf. *Characteristics of Men, Manners, Opinions, Times, etc.*, ed. John M. Robertson (London: Grant Richards, 1900), vol. II, pp. 171–2.

19. Stuart M. Tave, *The Amiable Humorists: A Study in the Comic Theory and Criticism of the Eighteenth and Early Nineteenth Centuries* (Chicago: Chicago University Press, 1960).

CHAPTER 4: A COCK AND BULL STORY

1. Cf. for the various connotations of gravity and *gravitas* Sigurd Burckhardt, '*Tristram Shandy*'s Law of Gravity', *ELH*, 28 (1961), 70–88; repr. in Melvyn New (ed.), '*Tristram Shandy': New Essays in Criticism* (London: Macmillan, 1992), 60–76.

2. William Holtz, 'Typography, Tristram Shandy: the Aposiopesis, etc.', in Arthur H. Cash and John M. Stedmond (eds.), *The Winged Skull: Papers from the Laurence Sterne Bicentenary Conference* (London: Methuen, 1971), 247–57; cf. also his *Image and Immortality: A Study of 'Tristram Shandy'* (Providence, RI: Brown University Press, 1970).

3. On an approximate count, more than one fifth of the chapters and an even higher percentage of pages is dedicated to Tristram's problems of writing his books; cf. William Freedman, *Laurence Sterne and the Origins of the Musical Novel* (Athens: University of Georgia Press, 1978), 28.

4. Cf. the more detailed statistics in Louis T. Milic, 'Information

Theory and the Style of *Tristram Shandy'*, in Arthur H. Cash and John M. Stedmond (eds.), *The Winged Skull*, 237–46.

5. Milic, 'Information Theory', 244.

6. E. M. Forster, *Aspects of the Novel* (London: Arnold, 1927), 164.

7. Alfred Einstein, *A Short History of Music* (New York: Vintage Books, 1957), 94; quoted from William Freedman, *Laurence Sterne and the Origins of the Musical Novel*, 15. My debt to Freedman here goes beyond this mere quotation. Cf. also Werner Wolf, *The Musicalization of Fiction: A Study in the Theory and History of Intermediality* (Amsterdam: Rodopi, 1999), 85–92.

8. Cf. on this structural contrast Rainer Warning, '*Tristram Shandy' und 'Jacques le Fataliste'* (München: Fink, 1965), 29.

9. Cf. Burckhardt, '*Tristram Shandy's* Law of Gravity', and Erwin Wolff, 'Falling and the Fall in Sterne's *Tristram Shandy'*, in Elmar Lehmann and Bernd Lenz (eds.), *Telling Stories: Studies in Honour of Ulrich Broich* (Amsterdam: B. R. Grüner, 1992), 97–108.

10. John Locke, *An Essay Concerning Human Understanding*, abridged and edited by John W. Yolton (London: Everyman, 1993), 269.

11. A particularly illuminating discussion of this dialogue is in John Traugott, *Tristram Shandy's World: Sterne's Philosophical Rhetoric* (Berkeley: University of California Press, 1954), 3–78; cf. also Ernest Lee Tuveson, 'Locke and Sterne', in J. A. Mazzeo (ed.), *Reason and the Imagination: Studies in the History of Ideas, 1600–1800* (New York: Columbia University Press, 1962), 255–77; Helen Moglen, *The Philosophical Irony of Laurence Sterne* (Gainesville: University of Florida Press, 1975), ch. 1; Peter M. Briggs, 'Locke's Essay and the Tentativeness of *Tristram Shandy'*, *Studies in Philology*, 82 (1985), 493–520; Wolfgang Iser, *Laurence Sternes 'Tristram Shandy': Inszenierte Subjektivität* (München: Fink, 1987), 11–50.

12. Cf. Louis A. Landa, 'The Shandean Homunculus: The Background of Sterne's Little Gentleman', in Carroll Camden (ed.), *Restoration and Eighteenth-Century Literature: Essays in Honor of Alan Dugal McKillop* (Chicago: University of Chicago Press, 1963), 49–68.

13. John Traugott, *Tristram Shandy's World: Sterne's Philosophical Rhetoric* (Berkeley: University of California Press, 1954), 7.

14. Sigmund Freud, *Zur Psychopathologie des Alltagslebens*, in *Gesammelte Werke* (Frankfurt: S. Fischer, 1969), vol. IV, 237–8.

15. Cf. the subtitle of Iser's study (above, note 11).

16. Cf. Jens Martin Gurr, '*Tristram Shandy' and the Dialectic of Enlightenment* (Heidelberg: C. Winter, 1999).

17. Jean Starobinski, *Montaigne: Denken und Existenz* (München: Hanser, 1986).

CHAPTER 5: ENGLISH TRANSPORTS AND FRENCH FRICTIONS

1. Jean-Jacques Rousseau, *Émile ou de l'éducation*, ed. François and Pierre Richard (Paris: Classiques Garnier, 1992), 580–81, 576–7. Cf. also Sterne's reflections on the Prodigal Son and 'the desire for travelling' in Melvyn New (ed.), *The Sermons*, vols. 4 and 5 (Gainesville: University of Florida Press, 1996), vol. 4, pp. 192–4.
2. Cf. his sermon 'Job's Account of the Shortness and Troubles of Life, considered' (*S* 99–100), the story of the 'the poor negro girl' in *Tristram Shandy* IX.vi or the exchange of letters with Ignatius Sancho, a self-educated negro born on board a slave-ship (*L* 282–7).
3. For recent work on the Grand Tour, cf. Christopher Hibbert, *The Grand Tour* (London: Methuen, 1987); Jeremy Black, *The Grand Tour in the Eighteenth Century* (Stroud: Sutton, 1992); Manfred Pfister (ed.), '*The Fatal Gift of Beauty': The Italies of British Travellers* (Amsterdam: Rodopi, 1996); Chloe Chard, *Pleasure and Guilt on the Grand Tour: Travel Writing and Imaginative Geography, 1600–1830* (Manchester: Manchester University Press, 1999).
4. Quoted from Pfister (ed.), '*The Fatal Gift of Beauty*', 78.
5. Tobias Smollett, quoted from Pfister, '*The Fatal Gift of Beauty*', 85–6.
6. Cf. Harry Sieber, *The Picaresque* (London: Methuen, 1977).
7. For a particularly vituperative critical view of Yorick, which turns *A Sentimental Journey* into one relentless satirical attack on sentimentalism, cf. Arthur Hill Cash, *Sterne's Comedy of Moral Sentiments: The Ethical Dimension of the 'Journey'* (Pittsburgh: Duquesne University Press, 1966).
8. Cf. Rufus Putney, 'The Evolution of *A Sentimental Journey*', *Philological Quarterly*, 19 (1940), 349–69.
9. Cf. Robert Markley, 'Sentimentality as Performance: Shaftesbury, Sterne, and the Theatrics of Virtue', in Felicity Nussbaum and Laura Brown (eds.), *The New Eighteenth Century: Theory, Politics, English Literature* (London: Methuen, 1987), 210–30.
10. *The Correspondence of Samuel Richardson*, ed. Anna Laetitia Barbauld (London: Richard Philips, 1804), vol. IV, pp. 282–3.
11. Cf. Ralph S. Crane, 'Suggestions Toward a Genealogy of "The Man of Feeling"', *English Literary History*, 1 (1934), 205–30.
12. Cf. Donald Greene, 'Latitudinarianism and Sensibility: The Genealogy of "The Man of Feeling" Reconsidered', *Modern Philology*, 75 (1977), 159–83 and Robert Markley, 'Sentimentality as Performance'.
13. Shaftesbury, quoted in Markley, 'Sentimentality as Performance', 213.

14. Markley, 'Sentimentality as Performance', 219.
15. Shaftesbury, *Characteristics of Men, Manners, Opinions, Times, etc.*, ed. John M. Robertson (London: Grant Richards, 1900), vol. II, p. 98.
16. *The Spectator*, Essay No. 565 (9 July 1714), ed. Gregory Smith (London: Dent, 1945), vol. IV, p. 282.
17. Anne Jessie Van Sant, *Eighteenth-Century Sensibility and the Novel: The Senses in Social Context* (Cambridge: Cambridge University Press, 1993), 100–101.
18. Virginia Woolf, 'The *Sentimental Journey*', in *The Common Reader, Second Series* (London: Hogarth Press, 1932), 78–85.
19. Cf. R. D. Mayo, *The English Novel in the Magazines, 1740–1815* (Oxford: Oxford University Press, 1962), *passim.*
20. Cf. Helmut Findeisen, 'Lorenzo-Kult in Seifersdorf', *Zeitschrift für Anglistik und Amerikanistik*, 6 (1958), 51–3; Lawrence Marsden Price, *English Literature in Germany* (Berkeley: University of California Press, 1953), ch. xv; cf. for an English translation of Jacobi's letter Alan B. Howes (ed.), *Sterne: The Critical Heritage* (London: Routledge & Kegan Paul, 1971), 429–31.
21. John Mullan, *Sentiment and Sociability: The Language of Feeling in the Eighteenth Century* (Oxford: Clarendon Press, 1988), 154.
22. Cf., with reference to *A Sentimental Journey*, Janet Todd, *Sensibility: An Introduction* (London: Methuen, 1986), 104–5.
23. Markley, 'Sentimentality as Performance', 229. I disagree here with Mark Loveridge's analysis of *A Sentimental Journey* as having a neat tripartite structure, which leads Yorick from learning French manners on the way to Paris to applying them in the city and finally becoming disenchanted with them in the countryside of southern France; cf. Mark Loveridge, *Laurence Sterne and the Argument About Design* (London: Methuen, 1982), 185.

Select Bibliography

BIBLIOGRAPHIES

Lodwick Hartley, *Laurence Sterne in the Twentieth Century: An Essay and a Bibliography of Sternean Studies, 1900–1965* (Chapel Hill: University of North Carolina Press, 1966).

———, *Laurence Sterne: An Annotated Bibliography, 1965–1977* (Boston: G. K. Hall, 1978).

Melvyn New, 'Surviving the Seventies: Sterne, Collins and Their Recent Critics', *Eighteenth-Century: Theory and Interpretation*, 25 (1984), 3–24.

EDITIONS OF WORKS BY LAURENCE STERNE

The Complete Works and Life of Laurence Sterne, ed. Wilbur L. Cross (New York: Taylor, 1904), 12 vols.

The Shakespeare Head Edition of the Writings of Laurence Sterne (Oxford: Blackwell, 1926–7), 7 vols.

The Florida Edition of the Works of Laurence Sterne, ed. Melvyn New et alii (Gainesville: University of Florida Press, 1978–).

The Life and Opinions of Tristam Shandy, Gentleman, ed. James A. Work (New York: Odyssey, 1940); ed. Ian Watt (Boston: Riverside Editions, 1965); ed. Graham Petrie (Harmondsworth: Penguin: 1967); ed. Melvyn New and Joan New, Florida Edition, vols. 1-3 (Gainesville: University of Florida Press, 1978–84); ed. Howard Anderson (New York: Norton, 1980); ed. Ian Cambell Ross (Oxford: World's Classics, 1983); ed. Melvyn and Joan New (Harmondsworth: Penguin, 1997).

A Sentimental Journey Through France and Italy, ed. Herbert Read (London: Scholartis Press, 1929); ed. Gardner D. Stout (Berkeley: University of California Press, 1967); ed. Graham Petrie (Harmondsworth: Penguin, 1967); *A Sentimental Journey through France and Italy, By Mr. Yorick* with *The Journal to Eliza* and *A Political Romance*, ed. Ian Jack (Oxford: Oxford University Press, 1968; Oxford: World's Classics, 1984).

The Sermons of Laurence Sterne, ed. Melvyn New, Florida Edition, vol. 4 (text), vol. 5 (notes) (Gainesville: University of Florida Press, 1996).

Letters of Laurence Sterne, ed. Lewis Perry Curtis (Oxford: Clarendon Press, 1935, 2nd edn 1965).

'Sterne's Rabelaisian Fragment: A Text from the Holograph Manuscript', ed. Melvyn New, *PMLA*, 87 (1972), 1083–92.

BIOGRAPHIES

Cash, Arthur H., *Laurence Sterne: The Early and Middle Years* (London: Methuen, 1975; London: Routledge, 1992).

——, *Laurence Sterne: The Later Years* (London: Methuen, 1986; London: Routledge, 1992).

Cross, Wilbur L., *Life and Times of Laurence Sterne* (New York: Macmillan, 1909; 3rd rev. edn New Haven: Yale University Press, 1929).

PERIODICALS

The Shandean: The Annual of the Laurence Sterne Trust (York: Laurence Sterne Trust, 1989–.

The Scriblerian (Philadelphia, PA: Temple University Press, 1968–71); since 1972 *The Scriblerian and the Kit-cats*; has included reviews of publications about Sterne since its Spring 1986 issue.

Eighteenth-Century: A Current Bibliography (London: AMS, 1928–).

ANTHOLOGIES OF CRITICISM AND ESSAY COLLECTIONS

Bloom, Harold (ed.), *Laurence Sterne's 'Tristram Shandy': Modern Critical Interpretations* (London: Chelsea House, 1987).

Cash, Arthur H. and John M. Stedmond (eds.), *The Winged Skull: Papers from the Laurence Sterne Bicentenary Conference* (London: Methuen, 1971).

Myer, Valerie Grosvenor (ed.), *Laurence Sterne: Riddles and Mysteries* (London: Vision, 1984).

New, Melvyn (ed.), *Approaches to Teaching Sterne's 'Tristram Shandy'* (New York: The Modern Language Association of America, 1989).

——,(ed.), *Laurence Sterne: 'Tristram Shandy': Contemporary Critical Essays*, New Casebooks (London: Macmillan, 1992).

——, (ed.), *Critical Essays on Laurence Sterne* (New York: G. K. Hall, 1998).

Rohmann, Gerd (ed.), *Laurence Sterne*, Wege der Forschung, 467 (Darmstadt: Wissenschaftliche Buchgesellschaft, 1980).

Traugott, John (ed.), *Laurence Sterne: A Collection of Critical Essays* (Englewood Cliffs, NJ: Prentice-Hall, 1968).

HISTORY OF RECEPTION: DIALOGUES WITH STERNE

Conrad, Peter, *Shandyism: The Character of Romantic Irony* (Oxford: Blackwell, 1978).

Fredman, Alice G., *Diderot and Sterne* (New York: Columbia University Press, 1955).

Hallamore, Gertrude Joyce, *Das Bild Laurence Sternes in Deutschland von der Aufklärung bis zur Romantik*, Germanische Studien, 1936 (Berlin, 1936; repr. Nendel: Kraus Reprint, 1967).

Hewett-Thayer, Harvey W., *Laurence Sterne in Germany* (New York: Columbia University Press, 1905).

Howes, Alan B., *Yorick and the Critics: Sterne's Reputation in England, 1760–1868* (New Haven: Yale University Press, 1958).

——, (ed.), *Sterne: The Critical Heritage* (London: Routledge & Kegan Paul, 1974).

Large, Duncan, ' "The Freest Writer": Nietzsche on Sterne', *The Shandean*, 7 (1995), 9–29.

Michelsen, Peter, *Laurence Sterne und der deutsche Roman des 18. Jahrhunderts* (Göttingen: Vandenhoeck, 1972).

Neubauer, John and Peter de Voogd (eds.), *The Reception of Laurence Sterne in Europe* (London: Athlone, in preparation).

Pierce, David and Peter de Voogd (eds.), *Laurence Sterne in Modernism and Postmodernism* (Amsterdam: Rodopi, 1996).

Pinger, W. R. R., *Laurence Sterne and Goethe* (Berkeley: University of California Press, 1920).

Price, Lawrence Marsden, *English Literature in Germany* (Berkeley: University of California Press, 1953), ch. xv.

Rabizzani, Giovanni, *Sterne in Italia* (Rome: Formiggini, 1920).

Santovetti, Olivia, 'The Adventurous Journey of Lorenzo Sterne in Italy', *The Shandean*, 8 (1996), 79–98.

CRITICAL BOOK-LENGTH STUDIES OF STERNE

Curtis, Lewis P., *The Politics of Laurence Sterne* (Oxford: Oxford University Press, 1929).

Fluchère, Henri, *Laurence Sterne, de l'homme à l'œuvre* (Paris: Gallimard, 1961).

———, *Laurence Sterne: From Tristram to Yorick*, trans. Barbara Bray (Oxford: Oxford University Press, 1965).

Freedman, William, *Laurence Sterne and the Origins of the Musical Novel* (Athens: University of Georgia Press, 1978).

Jefferson, D. W., *Laurence Sterne*, Writers and their Work (London: The British Council, 1954).

Kraft, Elizabeth, *Laurence Sterne Revisited* (New York: Twayne, 1996).

Lamb, Jonathan, *Sterne's Fiction and the Double Principle* (Cambridge: Cambridge University Press, 1989).

Loveridge, Mark, *Laurence Sterne and the Argument About Design* (Totowa, NJ: Barnes & Noble, 1982).

Moglen, Helen, *The Philosophical Irony of Laurence Sterne* (Gainesville: University of Florida Press, 1975).

Oates, J. C. T., *Shandyism and Sentiment* (Cambridge: Bibliographical Society, 1968).

Piper, William Bowman, *Laurence Sterne* (New York: Twayne, 1965).

Shaw, Margaret R. B., *Laurence Sterne: The Making of a Humorist, 1713–1762* (London: The Richards Press, 1957).

Stedmond, John M., *The Comic Art of Laurence Sterne: Convention and Innovation in 'Tristram Shandy' and 'A Sentimental Journey'* (Toronto: University of Toronto Press, 1967).

Traugott, John, *Tristram Shandy's World: Sterne's Philosophical Rhetoric* (Berkeley: University of California Press, 1954).

CRITICAL ESSAYS ON STERNE

Dyson, A. E., 'Sterne: The Novelist as Jester', *Critical Quarterly*, 4 (1962), 309–20.

Harries, Elizabeth W., 'Sterne's Novels: Gathering Up the Fragments', *English Literary History*, 49 (1982), 35–49.

Hartley, Lodwick, 'Sterne and the Eighteenth-Century Stage', *Papers in Language and Literature*, 4 (1968), 144–57.

Lamb, Jonathan, 'Sterne's System of Imitation', *Modern Language Review*, 76 (1981), 794–810.

Lukács, Georg, 'Reichtum, Chaos und Form – Ein Zwiegespräch über Laurence Sterne', in *Die Seele und die Formen* (Berlin: Fleischel, 1911; repr. Neuwied: Luchterhand, 1971), 265–323.

Mayoux, Jean-Jacques, 'Laurence Sterne parmi nous', *Critique*, 18, no. 177 (1962), 99–120.

Moss, Roger B., 'Sterne's Punctuation', *Eighteenth-Century Studies*, 15 (1981), 179–200.

Muir, Edwin, 'Laurence Sterne', in *Essays in Literature and Society* (London: Hogarth Press, 1949), 49–59.

Price, Martin, 'Sterne: Art and Nature', in *To the Palace of Wisdom: Studies in Order and Energy from Dryden to Blake* (New York: Doubleday, 1964), 313–42.

Putney, Rufus, 'Laurence Sterne: Apostle of Laughter', in James L. Clifford (ed.), *Eighteenth-Century English Literature* (London: Oxford University Press, 1959), 274–84.

Quennell, Peter, 'Laurence Sterne, the Novelist', in *Four Portraits: Studies of the Eighteenth Century* (London: Collins, 1945), 139–94.

Read, Herbert, 'Sterne's Sentimentality', in *The Sense of Glory: Essays in Criticism* (Cambridge: Cambridge University Press, 1929), 123–51.

Wehrs, Donald R., 'Sterne, Cervantes, Montaigne: Fideistic Scepticism and the Rhetoric of Desire', *Comparative Literature Studies*, 25 (1988), 127–51.

Woolf, Virginia, 'Sterne', in *Granite and Rainbow: Essays* (London: Hogarth Press, 1958), 169–80.

CRITICAL DISCUSSIONS OF *TRISTRAM SHANDY*

Anderson, Howard, 'Associationism and Wit in *Tristram Shandy*', *Philological Quarterly*, 48 (1969), 27–41.

——, '*Tristram Shandy* and the Reader's Imagination', *PMLA*, 86 (1971), 966–73.

Baird, Theodore, 'The Time-Scheme of *Tristram Shandy* and a Source', *PMLA*, 51 (1936), 803–20.

Benedict, B. M., '"Dear Madam": Rhetoric, Cultural Politics and the Female Reader in Sterne's *Tristram Shandy*', *Studies in Philology*, 89 (1992), 485–98.

Booth, Wayne C., 'Did Sterne Complete *Tristram Shandy*?', *Modern Philology*, 48 (1951), 172–83.

——, 'Telling as Showing: Dramatized Narrators, Reliable and Unreliable', in *The Rhetoric of Fiction* (Chicago: University of Chicago Press, 1961), 211–40.

Brady, Frank, '*Tristram Shandy*: Sexuality, Morality, and Sensibility', *Eighteenth-Century Studies*, 4 (1970), 41–56.

Briggs, Peter, 'Locke's *Essay* and the Tentativeness of *Tristram Shandy*', *Studies in Philology*, 82 (1985), 493–520.

Burckhardt, Sigurd, '*Tristram Shandy*'s Law of Gravity', *English Literary History*, 28 (1961), 70–88.

Byrd, Max, '*Tristram Shandy*' (London: George Allen & Unwin, 1987).

Cash, Arthur H., 'The Lockean Psychology of *Tristram Shandy*', *English Literary History*, 22 (1955), 125–35.

Ehlers, Leigh A., 'Mrs. Shandy's "Lint and Basilicon": The Importance of Women in *Tristram Shandy*', *South Atlantic Review*, 46:1 (1981), 61–75.

Ghent, Dorothy van, 'On *Tristram Shandy*', in *The English Novel: Form and Function* (New York: Rinehart, 1953), 104–22.

Gurr, Jens Martin, '*Tristram Shandy*' *and the Dialectic of Enlightenment* (Heidelberg: C. Winter, 1999).

Gysin, Fritz, *Model as Motif in 'Tristram Shandy'* (Berne: A. Francke, 1983).

Hillis Miller, John, 'Narrative Middles: A Preliminary Outline', *Genre*, 11 (1978), 375–87.

Holtz, William V., *Image and Immortality: A Study of 'Tristram Shandy'* (Providence, R. I.: Brown University Press, 1970).

Iser, Wolfgang, *Laurence Sternes 'Tristram Shandy': Inszenierte Subjektivität* (München: W. Fink, 1987).

——, *Laurence Sterne: 'Tristram Shandy'*, trans. David Henry Wilson (Cambridge: Cambridge University Press, 1988).

Jefferson, D. W., '*Tristram Shandy* and the Tradition of Learned Wit', *Essays in Criticism*, 1 (1951), 225–48.

Kerrigan, John, 'A Complete History of Comic Noses', in Michael Cordner, Peter Holland and John Kerrigan (eds.), *English Comedy* (Cambridge: Cambridge University Press, 1994), 241–66.

King, Ross, '*Tristram Shandy* and the Wound of Language', *Studies in Philology*, 92 (1995), 291–310.

Landa, Louis A., 'The Shandean Homunculus: The Background of Sterne's "Little Gentleman"', in Carroll Camden (ed.), *Restoration and Eighteenth-Century Literature: Essays in Honor of Alan Dugald McKillop* (Chicago: University of Chicago Press, 1963), 49–68.

Lanham, Richard A., '*Tristram Shandy': The Games of Pleasure* (Berkeley: University of California Press, 1973).

Lehman, Benjamin H., 'Of Time, Personality, and the Author: A Study of *Tristram Shandy*', in *Studies in the Comic* (Berkeley: California University Press, 1941), 233–50.

Markley, Robert, '*Tristram Shandy* and "Narrative Middles": Hillis Miller and the Style of Deconstructive Criticism', *Genre*, 17 (1984), 179–90.

McMaster, Juliet, 'Walter Shandy, Sterne, and Gender: A Feminist Foray', *English Studies in Canada*, 15 (1989), 441–58.

Mendilow, A. A., 'The Revolt of Sterne', in *Time and the Novel* (London: Peter Nevill, 1952), 158–99.

Moglen, Helen, '(W)holes and Noses: The Indeterminacies of *Tristram Shandy*', *Literature and Psychology*, 41:3 (1995), 44–79.

New, Melvyn, *Laurence Sterne as Satirist: A Reading of 'Tristram Shandy'* (Gainesville: University of Florida Press, 1969).

——, 'Sterne, Warburton, and the Burden of Exuberant Wit', *Eighteenth-Century Studies*, 15 (1982), 245–74.

——, '*Tristram Shandy': A Book for Free Spirits* (New York: Twayne, 1994).

Oakleaf, David, 'Long Sticks, Morris Dancers, and Gentlemen:

Associations of the Hobby-horse in *Tristram Shandy*, *Eighteenth-Century Life*, 11 (1987), 62–76.

Ostovich, Helen, 'Reader as Hobby-Horse in *Tristram Shandy*', *Philological Quarterly*, 68 (1989), 325–42.

Park, William, '*Tristram Shandy* and the New Novel of Sensibility', *Studies in the Novel*, 6 (1974), 268–79.

Parnell, Tim, 'A Story Painted to the Heart? *Tristram Shandy* and Sentimentalism Reconsidered', *The Shandean*, 9 (1997), 122–35.

Rogers, Pat, 'Tristram Shandy's Polite Conversation', *Essays in Criticism*, 32 (1982), 303–20.

Rosenblum, Michael, 'The Sermon, the King of Bohemia, and the Art of Interpolation in *Tristram Shandy*', *Studies in Philology*, 75 (1978), 472–91.

Shklovsky, Viktor, 'Sterne's *Tristram Shandy*: A Stylistic Commentary', in Lee T. Lemon and Marion J. Reis (eds.), *Russian Formalist Criticism: Four Essays* (Lincoln: University of Nebraska Press, 1965), 25–57.

——, 'A Parodying Novel: Sterne's *Tristram Shandy*', in John Traugott (ed.), *Laurence Sterne: A Collection of Critical Essays* (Englewood Cliffs, NJ: Prentice-Hall, 1968), 66–89.

Stanzel, Franz, '*Tom Jones* and *Tristram Shandy*', *English Miscellany*, 5 (1954), 107–48.

Swearingen, James E., *Reflexivity in 'Tristram Shandy': An Essay in Phenomenological Criticism* (New Haven, CT: Yale University Press, 1977).

Warning, Rainer, *Illusion und Wirklichkeit in 'Tristram Shandy' and 'Jacques le Fataliste'* (München: W. Fink, 1965).

Whittaker, Ruth, '*Tristram Shandy*' (Milton Keynes: Open University Press, 1988).

Wolff, Erwin, 'Falling and the Fall in *Tristram Shandy*', in Elmar Lehmann and Bernd Lenz (eds.), *Telling Stories: Studies in Honour of Ulrich Broich* (Amsterdam: B. R. Grüner, 1992), 97–108.

Zander, Horst, '"Non Enim Adjectio Ejus Sed Opus Ipsum Est": Überlegungen zum Paratext in *Tristram Shandy*', *Poetica*, 28 (1996), 132–53.

Zimmerman, Everett, '*Tristram Shandy* and Narrative Representation', *The Eighteenth Century: Theory and Interpretation*, 28 (1987), 127–47.

CRITICAL DISCUSSIONS OF *A SENTIMENTAL JOURNEY*

Cash, Arthur H., *Sterne's Comedy of Moral Sentiments: The Ethical Dimension of the 'Journey'* (Pittsburgh: Duquesne University Press, 1966).

Davidson, Arnold A. and Cathy N., 'Yorick contra Hobbes: Comic

Synthesis in Sterne's *A Sentimental Journey*', *Centennial Review*, 21 (1977), 282–93.

Denizot, Paul, 'Yorick et la quête du bonheur; Ou, Les Equivoques ludiques du corps et de l'âme dans *A Sentimental Journey*', in P. G. Boucé and S. Halimi (eds.), *Le corps et l'âme en Grande Bretagne au XVIIIe siècle* (Paris: Sorbonne, 1986), 157–66.

Dilworth, Ernest N., *The Unsentimental Journey of Laurence Sterne* (Morningside Heights, NY: King's Crown Press, 1948).

Fairer, David, 'Sentimental Translation in Mackenzie and Sterne', *Essays in Criticism*, 49 (1999), 132–51.

Frank, Judith, ' "A Man who laughs is never Dangerous": Character and Class in Sterne's *A Sentimental Journey*', *English Literary History*, 56 (1989), 97–124.

Gould, Rebecca, 'Sterne's Sentimental Yorick as Male Hysteric', *Studies in English Literature, 1500–1900*, 36 (1996), 641–53.

Lamb, Jonathan, 'Language and Hartleian Associationism in *A Sentimental Journey*', *Eighteenth-Century Studies*, 5 (1971), 243–55.

MacLean, Kenneth, 'Imagination and Sympathy: Sterne and Adam Smith', *Journal of the History of Ideas*, 10 (1949), 399–410.

Markley, Robert, 'Sentimentality as Performance: Shaftesbury, Sterne, and the Theatrics of Virtue', in Felicity Nussbaum and Laura Brown (eds.), *The New Eighteenth Century: Theory, Politics, English Literature* (London: Methuen, 1987), 210–30.

Putney, Rufus, 'The Evolution of *A Sentimental Journey*', *Philological Quarterly*, 19 (1940), 349–69.

Sedgwick, Eve Kosofsky, '*A Sentimental Journey*: Sexualism and the Citizen of the World', in *Between Men: English Literature and Male Homosexual Desire* (New York: Columbia University Press, 1985), 67–82.

Seidel, Michael, 'Narrative Crossings: Sterne's *A Sentimental Journey*', *Genre*, 18 (1985), 1–22.

Smitten, Jeffrey, 'Gesture and Expression in Eighteenth-Century Fiction: *A Sentimental Journey*', *Modern Language Studies*, 9:3 (1979), 85–97.

Stout Jr., Gardner, 'Yorick's *Sentimental Journey*: A Comic "Pilgrim's Progress" for the Man of Feeling', *English Literary History*, 30 (1963), 395–412.

Woolf, Virginia, 'The *Sentimental Journey*', in *The Common Reader: Second Series* (London: Hogarth Press, 1932), 78-85.

LITERARY, INTELLECTUAL AND SOCIAL CONTEXTS

Alter, Robert, *The Novel as a Self-Conscious Genre* (Berkeley: University of

California Press, 1975).

Barrel, John, *English Literature in History, 1730–1780* (London: Hutchinson, 1983).

Barker-Benfield, G. J., *The Culture of Sensibility: Sex and Society in Eighteenth-Century England* (Chicago: University of Chicago Press, 1992).

Bellamy, Liz, *Commerce, Morality and the Eighteenth-Century Novel* (Cambridge: Cambridge University Press, 1998).

Benedict, Barbara, *Framing Feeling: Sentiment and Style in English Prose Fiction 1745–1800* (New York: AMS Press, 1994).

Booth, Wayne C., 'The Self-Conscious Narrator in Comic Fiction before *Tristram Shandy*', *PMLA*, 67 (1952), 163–85.

Bredvold, Louis I., *The Natural History of Sensibility* (Detroit: Wayne State University Press, 1962).

Brissenden, R. F., *Virtue in Distress: Studies in the Novel of Sentiment from Richardson to Sade* (London: Hutchinson, 1951).

Browne, Alice, *The Eighteenth-Century Feminist Mind* (Brighton: Harvester, 1987).

Busch, Werner, *Das sentimentalische Bild: Die Krise der Kunst im 18. Jahrhundert und die Geburt der Moderne* (München, Beck: 1993).

Chard, Chloe, *Pleasure and Guilt on the Grand Tour: Travel Writing and Imaginative Geography, 1600–1830* (Manchester: Manchester University Press, 1999).

Cohen, Michèle, *Fashioning Masculinity: National Identity and Language in the Eighteenth Century* (London: Routledge, 1996).

Cragg, Gerald R., *The Church and the Age of Reason, 1648–1789* (New York: Atheneum, 1961).

Crane, Ralph Stephen, 'Suggestions Toward a Genealogy of the "Man of Feeling"', *English Literary History*, 1 (1934), 205–30.

Doody, Margaret Anne, *A Natural Passion* (Oxford: Clarendon Press, 1974).

Downey, James, *The Eighteenth-Century Pulpit: A Study of the Sermons of Butler, Berkeley, Secker, Sterne, Whitefield and Wesley* (Oxford: Clarendon Press, 1969).

Dussinger, J. A., *The Discourse of the Mind in Eighteenth-Century Fiction* (The Hague: Mouton, 1974).

Ellis, Markman, *The Politics of Sensibility: Race, Gender and Commerce in the Sentimental Novel* (Cambridge: Cambridge University Press, 1996).

Erickson, Robert A., *Mother Midnight: Birth, Sex, and Fate in Eighteenth-Century Fiction* (New York: AMS Press, 1986).

Friedman, Arthur, 'Aspects of Sentimentalism in Eighteenth-Century Literature', in Henry Knight Miller, Eric Rothstein and G. S. Rousseau (eds.), *The Augustan Milieu: Essays Presented to Louis A. Landa* (Oxford: Clarendon Press, 1970), 247–61.

119

Frye, Northrop, 'Towards Defining an Age of Sensibility', *English Literary History*, 23 (1956), 144–52.

——, *Anatomy of Criticism: Four Essays* (Princeton, NJ: Princeton University Press, 1957).

Greene, Donald, 'Latitudinarianism and Sensibility: The Genealogy of the "Man of Feeling" Reconsidered', *Modern Philology*, 75 (1977), 159–83.

Harries, Elizabeth, *The Unfinished Manner: Essays on the Fragment in the Later Eighteenth Century* (Charlottesville: University Press of Virginia, 1994).

Hutcheon, Linda, *Narcissistic Narrative: The Metafictional Paradox* (London: Methuen, 1984).

Jäger, Georg, *Empfindsamkeit und Roman* (Stuttgart: Metzler, 1969).

Kay, Carol, *Political Constructions: Defoe, Richardson, and Sterne in Relation to Hobbes, Hume, and Burke* (Ithaca, NY: University of Cornell Press, 1988).

Kraft, Elizabeth, *Character and Consciousness in Eighteenth-Century Comic Fiction* (Athens: University of Georgia Press, 1992).

London, April, *Women and Property in the Eighteenth-Century Novel* (Cambridge: Cambridge University Press, 1999).

Mayo, R. D., *The English Novel in the Magazines, 1740–1815* (Oxford: Oxford University Press, 1962).

McGann, Jerome, *The Poetics of Sensibility: A Revolution in Literary Style* (Oxford: Clarendon Press, 1996).

McKillop, Alan Dugald, *The Early Masters of English Fiction* (Lawrence: University of Kansas Press, 1956).

Mileur, Jean-Pierre, 'Revisionism, Irony and the Mask of Sentiment', *New Literary History*, 29 (1998), 197–233.

Mullan, John, *Sentiment and Sociability: The Language of Feeling in the Eighteenth Century* (Oxford: Clarendon Press, 1988).

Nisbet, H.B., and Claude Rawson (eds.), *The Cambridge History of Literary Criticism*, vol. IV, *The Eighteenth Century* (Cambridge: Cambridge University Press, 1997).

Nussbaum, Felicity, and Laura Brown (eds.), *The New Eighteenth Century: Theory, Politics, English Literature* (London: Methuen, 1987).

Nuttall, A. D., *A Common Sky: Philosophy and the Literary Imagination* (London: Chatto & Windus, 1974).

Paulson, Ronald, *Satire and the Novel in Eighteenth-Century England* (New Haven, CT: Yale University Press, 1967).

Pfister, Manfred (ed.), *'The Fatal Gift of Beauty': The Italies of British Travellers* (Amsterdam: Rodopi, 1996).

Preston, John, *The Created Self: The Reader's Role in Eighteenth-Century Fiction* (London: Heinemann, 1970).

Richetti, John, *The Cambridge Companion to the Eighteenth Century*

(Cambridge: Cambridge University Press, 1996).

Rogers, Katharine, *Feminism in Eighteenth-Century England* (Urbana: University of Illinois Press, 1982).

Rothstein, Eric, *Systems of Order and Inquiry in Later Eighteenth-Century Fiction* (Berkeley: University of California Press, 1975).

Rousseau, G. S., 'Nerves, Spirits and Fibres: Towards the Origin of Sensibility', in R. F. Brissenden (ed.), *Studies in the Eighteenth Century III* (Canberra: Australian National University Press, 1975), 137–57.

Seidel, Michael, *Satiric Inheritance from Rabelais to Sterne* (Princeton: Princeton University Press, 1979).

Sheriff, John K., *The Good-Natured Man: The Evolution of a Moral Ideal, 1660–1800* (University, AL: University of Alabama Press, 1982).

Sitter, John, *Literary Loneliness in Mid-Eighteenth-Century England* (Ithaca: Cornell University Press, 1982).

Spacks, Patricia Meyer, *Imagining a Self: Autobiography and Novel in Eighteenth-Century England* (Cambridge, MA: Harvard University Press, 1976).

Tave, Stuart M., *The Amiable Humorist: A Study in the Comic Theory and Criticism of the Eighteenth and Early Nineteenth Centuries* (Chicago: University of Chicago Press, 1960).

Todd, Janet, *Sensibility: An Introduction* (London: Methuen, 1986).

Tuveson, Ernest Lee, 'Locke and Sterne', in J. A. Mazzeo (ed.), *Reason and the Imagination: Studies in the History of Ideas, 1600–1800* (New York: Columbia University Press, 1962), 255–77.

Van Sant, Ann Jessie, *Eighteenth-Century Sensibility and the Novel: The Senses in Social Context* (Cambridge: Cambridge University Press, 1993).

Wolf, Werner, 'The Language of Feeling between Transparency and Opacity: The Semiotics of the English Eighteenth-Century Novel', in Wilhelm G. Busse (ed.), *Anglistentag 1991* (Tübingen: Niemeyer, 1992), 108–29.

———, *The Musicalization of Fiction: A Study in the Theory and History of Intermediality* (Amsterdam: Rodopi, 1999).

Index

*Recent and
Forthcoming Titles
in the
New Series of*

WRITERS AND
THEIR WORK

*"...this series promises to outshine its own
previously high reputation."*
Times Higher Education Supplement

*"...will build into a fine multi-volume critical
encyclopaedia of English literature."*
Library Review & Reference Review

"...Excellent, informative, readable, and recommended."
NATE News

*"written by outstanding contemporary critics,
whose expertise is flavoured by unashamed enthusiasm for
their subjects and the series' diverse aspirations."*
Times Educational Supplement

*"A useful and timely addition to the ranks of the lit crit and
reviews genre. Written in an accessible and authoritative style."*
Library Association Record

WRITERS AND THEIR WORK

RECENT & FORTHCOMING TITLES

Title	Author
Peter Ackroyd	*Susana Onega*
Kingsley Amis	*Richard Bradford*
Anglo-Saxon Verse	*Graham Holderness*
Antony and Cleopatra	*Ken Parker*
As You Like It	*Penny Gay*
W. H. Auden	*Stan Smith*
Alan Ayckbourn	*Michael Holt*
J. G. Ballard	*Michel Delville*
Djuna Barnes	*Deborah Parsons*
Aphra Behn 2/e	*Sue Wiseman*
John Betjeman	*Dennis Brown*
Edward Bond	*Michael Mangan*
Anne Brontë	*Betty Jay*
Emily Brontë	*Stevie Davies*
A. S. Byatt	*Richard Todd*
Byron	*Drummond Bone*
Caroline Drama	*Julie Sanders*
Angela Carter	*Lorna Sage*
Geoffrey Chaucer	*Steve Ellis*
Children's Literature	*Kimberley Reynolds*
Caryl Churchill 2/e	*Elaine Aston*
John Clare	*John Lucas*
S. T. Coleridge	*Stephen Bygrave*
Joseph Conrad	*Cedric Watts*
Crime Fiction	*Martin Priestman*
Shashi Deshpande	*Armrita Bhalla*
Charles Dickens	*Rod Mengham*
John Donne	*Stevie Davies*
Carol Ann Duffy 2/e	*Deryn Rees Jones*
Early Modern Sonneteers	*Michael Spiller*
George Eliot	*Josephine McDonagh*
English Translators of Homer	*Simeon Underwood*
Henry Fielding	*Jenny Uglow*
Veronica Forrest-Thomson – Language Poetry	*Alison Mark*
E. M. Forster	*Nicholas Royle*
Elizabeth Gaskell	*Kate Flint*
The *Gawain*-Poet	*John Burrow*
The Georgian Poets	*Rennie Parker*
William Golding	*Kevin McCarron*
Graham Greene	*Peter Mudford*
Ivor Gurney	*John Lucas*
Hamlet	*Ann Thompson & Neil Taylor*
Thomas Hardy	*Peter Widdowson*
David Hare	*Jeremy Ridgman*
Tony Harrison	*Joe Kelleher*
William Hazlitt	*J. B. Priestley; R. L. Brett (intro. by Michael Foot)*
Seamus Heaney 2/e	*Andrew Murphy*
George Herbert	*T.S. Eliot (intro. by Peter Porter)*
Henrik Ibsen	*Sally Ledger*
Kazuo Ishiguro	*Cynthia Wong*

RECENT & FORTHCOMING TITLES

TITLES IN PREPARATION

Title	Author
Chinua Achebe	*Nahem Yousaf*
Ama Ata Aidoo	*Nana Wilson-Tagoe*
Matthew Arnold	*Kate Campbell*
Margaret Atwood	*Marion Wynne-Davies*
Jane Austen	*Robert Miles*
John Banville	*Peter Dempsey*
Pat Barker	*Sharon Monteith*
Julian Barnes	*Matthew Pateman*
Samuel Beckett	*Keir Elam*
William Blake	*Steven Vine*
Elizabeth Bowen	*Maud Ellmann*
Charlotte Brontë	*Patsy Stoneman*
Robert Browning	*John Woodford*
John Bunyan	*Tamsin Spargoe*
Cymbeline	*Peter Swaab*
Daniel Defoe	*Jim Rigney*
Anita Desai	*Elaine Ho*
Shashi Deshpande	*Amrita Bhalla*
Margaret Drabble	*Glenda Leeming*
John Dryden	*David Hopkins*
T. S. Eliot	*Colin MacCabe*
J. G. Farrell	*John McLeod*
John Fowles	*William Stephenson*
Brian Friel	*Geraldine Higgins*
Athol Fugard	*Dennis Walder*
Nadine Gordimer	*Lewis Nkosi*
Geoffrey Grigson	*R. M. Healey*
Neil Gunn	*J. B. Pick*
Geoffrey Hill	*Andrew Roberts*
Gerard Manley Hopkins	*Daniel Brown*
Ted Hughes	*Susan Bassnett*
Samuel Johnson	*Liz Bellamy*
Ben Jonson	*Anthony Johnson*
John Keats	*Kelvin Everest*
James Kelman	*Gustav Klaus*
Rudyard Kipling	*Jan Montefiore*
Charles and Mary Lamb	*Michael Baron*
Wyndham Lewis	*Andrzej Gasiorak*
Malcolm Lowry	*Hugh Stevens*
Macbeth	*Kate McCluskie*
Katherine Mansfield	*Andrew Bennett*
Una Marson & Louise Bennett	*Alison Donnell*
Merchant of Venice	*Warren Chernaik*
John Milton	*Jonathan Sawday*
Bharati Mukherjee	*Manju Sampat*
Alice Munro	*Ailsa Cox*
R. K. Narayan	*Shirley Chew*
New Women Novelists of the Late 19th Century	*Gail Cunningham*
Grace Nichols	*Sarah Lawson-Welsh*
Ben Okri	*Robert Fraser*
Caryl Phillips	*Helen Thomas*
Religious Poets of the 17th Century	*Helen Wilcox*

TITLES IN PREPARATION

Title	Author
Revenge Tragedy	*Janet Clare*
Samuel Richardson	*David Deeming*
Nayantara Sahgal	*Ranjana Ash*
Sam Selvon	
Sir Walter Scott	*Harriet Harvey-Wood*
Mary Shelley	*Catherine Sharrock*
Charlotte Smith & Helen Williams	*Angela Keane*
Stevie Smith	*Martin Gray*
R. L. Stevenson	*David Robb*
Gertrude Stein	*Nicola Shaughnessy*
Bram Stoker	*Andrew Maunder*
Tom Stoppard	*Nicholas Cadden*
Jonathan Swift	*Ian Higgins*
Algernon Swinburne	*Catherine Maxwell*
The Tempest	*Gordon McMullan*
Tennyson	*Seamus Perry*
W. M. Thackeray	*Richard Salmon*
Three Avant-Garde Poets	*Peter Middleton*
Derek Walcott	*Stephen Regan*
Marina Warner	*Laurence Coupe*
Jeanette Winterson	*Margaret Reynolds*
Women Romantic Poets	*Anne Janowitz*
Women Writers of the 17th Century	*Ramona Wray*
Women Writers at the Fin de Siècle	*Angelique Richardson*